Cultural Defiance, Cultural Deviance

Collected Essays

Peter K. Fallon

SophiaOmni

ISBN: 978-1482696516

SophiaOmni

Visit our website at:
www.sophiaomni.org

This book is dedicated, with love, to my children

Christine Ceilí Fallon,
Brigid Caitlín Fallon,
and
Brendan Conor Fallon

CONTENTS

Acknowledgements

This slim volume of essays came as something of a surprise to me. It was not on my radar, not on my "to do" list. On the contrary, I was trying to finish a couple of other research and writing projects in the Spring of 2012 when Dr. Michael S Russo of the Center for Social and Ethical Concerns at Molloy College suggested to me that putting together a collection of brief essays on a disparate selection of topics was a good idea rather than a trifle. I was not initially persuaded by his arguments (a piece of me remains fairly skeptical even now), but his persistence and intensity eventually won the day. At any rate, I wish to acknowledge my gratitude to Dr. Russo for his support as well as for our nearly two-decade-long friendship. He is as good a friend to me as he is a teacher and mentor to his students. And that is saying a lot.

I would be completely remiss if I failed to acknowledge the love and support of my friend (and wife) Dr. Mary Pat Fallon of the Graduate School of Library and Information Sciences at Dominican University. Mary Pat and Mike Russo conspired to goad me and prod me into believing that people – outside of a very few like-minded deontologists at academic conferences and scholarly colloquia – might actually be interested in reading the counter-cultural thoughts of (a fellow many consider – incorrectly, I hope – to be) a "Luddite" and "curmudgeon." As she has on so many occasions in the past, Mary Pat encouraged me to put my thoughts on paper and take "the leap of faith," in spite of my years of experience that much of the seed I yearn to sow falls on barren ground (Mark 4:4-7). She reminded me that if something is worth doing, it is worth doing *in, of, and for itself* and not for any particular desired outcome. I must also, then, acknowledge her patience with me during the many tedious months of editing, revision, and production. I am honored and blessed to have such a friend.

While they were not directly involved in the process of creating this book, another small group of people deserve my gratitude. The Dominican Sisters of Sinsinawa, particularly those of Rosary Convent, have been my family for the last decade and more. While all the Sisters deservedly share my eternal gratitude for their friendship, love and support, three have had a profound impact on my thoughts and work, and our conversations over coffee or around the dinner table have constituted for me a process of continuous and continual formation – intellectual as well as spiritual – of the person I am. Sisters Melissa Waters, O.P., Jeanne Crapo, O.P., and Clemente Davlin, O.P. have graciously listened to me over several years as I put forward many of the arguments that appear in this book, and responded in the most helpful, constructive, and affirming ways. They simultaneously listened to me and instructed me, agreed with me and (gently) directed me, supported me and inspired me to see beyond the artificial boundaries of a culture far more willing to hide from, than confront, social ills. They are and have been, and will always be, a source of strength to me.

Finally, in the interests of clarity and realism, but also in the hopes of encouraging others in my position, others who feel the need to raise public objection to the idea that our amazing technological developments of recent decades constitute "progress" when poverty, ignorance, racism, exploitation, and a host of other human failures not only persist but grow and spread, I want to acknowledge what we – the cultural minority, the defiant, the deviant – are up against. Academia is becoming a business rationalized by market values. Administrators, I believe, are more and more concerned with "marketability" and the "competitive edge" than they are with the formation of good people: people of values, people of conscience, people of concern for the common good. Faculty and staff are under enormous economic pressure to conform to new modes of thought and assimilate market principles not only into their own administrative procedures but into their pedagogy and even their curricula. Scholarship itself risks becoming – if it has not already become – an industry in the service of the economy rather than a human activity inherently good in, of, and for itself. I feel the need to acknowledge, here, in this book, on this page, the powerful influence this new orientation has had on my thinking and my work, how it has provoked in me the urge to become, in Neil Postman's words, a "loving resistance fighter" against the goals and values of Jacques Ellul's "technological society": efficiency, profit, marketability, ease, convenience, speed, etc.

And so I also feel the need to acknowledge, for the sake of the few loving resistance fighters who find themselves reading this, that applied research is indeed a form of scholarship. But it is *a* form, not *the* form. Theoretical and critical research – including ethics – is a form of scholarship not only of equal value to applied research, but at times a superior form. And I believe firmly we are living through such a time right now. Therefore, finally, I wish to acknowledge the encouragement and understanding of a handful of colleagues at Roosevelt University who have allowed themselves to see beyond the constraints of these new attitudes toward higher education, even as they labor under their burden: Anne-Marie Cusac, Charles Madigan, and Mary Ellen Schiller. You have my thanks.

Foreword
Fishing in the Clouds:
Ten Essays for the Seriously Curious

When the torrent sweeps a man against a boulder, you must expect him to scream, and you need not be surprised if the scream is sometimes a theory.[1]

Your greatest strength is always simultaneously your greatest weakness, and one of the great and terrible appeals of the interdisciplinary field of media ecology is that its members are interested in absolutely everything. Peter K. Fallon, author of the book you are now holding, is no exception.

Neil Postman once remarked on this phenomenon as we walked back from lunch in Greenwich Village, and pushed open the glass doors of The Department of Culture and Communication on the seventh floor of NYU's Steinhardt School of Education building. Speaking verbally and audibly, Postman said, "We named it 'The Department of Culture and Communication' because it includes everything. What does it leave out? It's like calling it 'The Department of Man and Woman.'"

In an interview conducted verbally and transcribed by Colleen Carroll Campbell for *The St. Louis Post Dispatch* for an article that is now no longer searchable on the paper's official website archive, Walter Ong once said his research interest was "anything that lives." I swear to you he said that. I just don't have the citation. A colleague of Ong's in that same piece compared him to "a walking encyclopedia."

In his written essay, "Needed: A New Karl Marx!", the

great polymath Jacques Ellul commented on the need for such an encyclopedic interest.

> First of all, it is necessary to know the ensemble of the phenomena, to have an encyclopedic view of our time. This assumes an obvious superficiality. However, by no means can it be an incoherent knowledge or a mixture without order...*This encyclopedism is absolutely necessary, since no specialization will permit one to take into account the questions of our civilization.*[2] (emphasis mine)

Marshall McLuhan – whose son Eric coined the term *media ecology* before Neil Postman first uttered it publicly on Sunday, November 24, 1968 – said a similar thing:

> "The wired planet has no boundaries and no monopolies of knowledge. The affairs of the world are now dependent upon the highest information of which man is capable...The boundaries between the world of affairs and the community of learning have ceased to exist. The workaday world now demands encyclopedic wisdom."

You can find this on a Google search, so it must be true. McLuhan wrote twenty books, and took the academic imperative *publish or perish* to a whole new level by writing almost half of these books after he died. Neil Postman wrote nearly twenty books. Walter Ong wrote ten books. Jacques Ellul wrote fifty-eight books, the majority of which have still never been translated from French.

To the names of McLuhan, Postman, Ellul, and Ong, please now add Peter K. Fallon. This isn't so much a book as it is a placeholder for polymaths. This isn't a collection of essays unified by a theme or subject, but rather a collection of discrete objects subjected to the same methodology. They are historical, analogical, probing, semantic, linguistic, and psychological.

And not religious but spiritual, in the best sense of that beaten dead horse.

This book takes its title from the lead essay, which is misleading but ultimately helpful. The second and tenth essays are on subjects that will have become obsolete by the time you read this in print: The Occupy Movement? Trayvon Martin? Historic events of cultural significance that took place more than five minutes ago are, unfortunately, *so five minutes ago* in public perception. But at the time, when these pieces were given as oral messages to a live audience in hearing range of the speaker, they were absolutely up to the minute. The medium still is the message, and the medium of print is really just a museum for the medium of speech, so you'll have to forgive the non-tweeted-live nature of these pieces. Likewise the dictionary is just a cemetery for dead metaphors, which is why gangsta rap is practically the only place for fresh metaphors nowadays, and there's no getting around the fact that this thing you're holding is a book, and not a YouTube video with a stack of connected and clickable links on the right-hand column. Seriously: I'm sorry about that. They would make excellent YouTube videos. In fact, if you do a YouTube search on "Peter Fallon," make sure you click on the first few videos, and not the later ones, which involve a poet with the same name who looks suspiciously like an Irishman speaking English, and like the kind of guy you'd find hanging around O'Neill's Pub on Anne Street in Dublin looking for a free pint of Guinness. Maybe it will help to read these essays out loud to yourself with the AutoTune app on your iPhone right up against your vocal chords. I know how daunting reading can be these days, and my name *is Read*. I know it's a lot more like solitary confinement than the soul's liberation it used to be. When the ground shifts, the figures topple.

Did you ever see that guy with the Smart Car wearing SmartWool socks drinking SmartWater munching on his SmartFood popcorn while working on his SmartPad at IBM in order to build a smarter planet? You just knew this guy was an idiot the minute you saw him, because subconsciously you perceived him as a total tool – a victim of the unconsciousness engendered by the media and technology all around him. He thinks he is most free when he is in fact most enslaved. He perceives himself to be the smartest in the eyes of others precisely at the point when he looks and acts the dumbest. His plight is described in Chapter Three, and it's worth the deferred gratification you'll have to acquire to get through it, because it is way longer than 144 characters. That's four more than Twitter actually allows, but is a far more satisfying and symbolic number.

Did you know that the Eucharist is a figure that defines the user's relationship to God on the ground of belief or disbelief? It is, and the discussion in Chapters Two and Six are enlightening on many aspects of why the modern media and the ancient mass have more in common than you might otherwise suspect.

Are you interested in finding out who Peter K. Fallon is? He's interviewed in Chapter Four, and in Chapters Five and Nine he interviews Postman and McLuhan as well, even though he's not technically with them when he does so, and neither are they. That's okay, because disembodiment is one of the primary effects of digital media, so they don't have to be there in person in order to be there in spirit.

How does that work? As of 2005, you've got the cloud to look it up. *The cloud* is short for what we now call *cloud computing*. It's where all of human consciousness is located nowadays, the externalized, collective, historical content of all human thought that was once located in individual brains and later in specific libraries. *The cloud* is really just the replacement term for what William Gibson called *cyberspace* in 1984 (okay, 1982 if you're a purist). Gibson's term *cyber* evokes *cypher* or negative space. Interestingly, *mostly* digital people are *mostly* agnostic or atheist. And mostly digital people, when asked to describe God, come up with these three terms most often: *oblong, grey, blur*. In other words: God is pretty cloud-like to a lot of people. The parts of a Christian's brain that light up when they think about Jesus is the same part that lights up when you think about your iPhone. The guy who wrote that in a letter to the editors of *Christianity Today* couldn't provide the citation when I asked him for it, but he stood by it. But Fallon performs his imaginary interviews by pulling from a deeper cloud with a longer tradition, one that an author writing with Authority described in AD 63 as *"a great cloud of witnesses."* In this collection, Fallon has inducted McLuhan and Postman into his own personal cloud of great witnesses, only slightly ahead of the Catholic Church, in McLuhan's case, and the Rabbinical School of Media Mysticism in Postman's case. The former of these is real but made McLuhan an "intellectual suicide" among his University of Toronto colleagues in his own day. The latter of these is something I just made up because Postman was a Jewish New Yorker who was not really classifiable by any given orthodoxy (that I'm aware of, at least). Postman did at one point say that he didn't know if God had spoken or not, but he lived his life as though He had, because he feared that if he did not, he would lose his way. But in both cases, McLuhan and Postman were truly "outsiders" to the dominant homogeneity of their intellectual environments, and this was one of the primary reasons why they were so good at perceiving the media environments of their day. *We don't know who discovered water*, McLuhan liked to say (quoting Ted Carpenter, quoting John Culkin, who was paraphrasing a bit of ancient Chinese wisdom), *but we're certain it wasn't a fish*. In fact, as you might have guessed, a fish only perceives that water is a medium it lives and breathes and has its being in when it becomes a fish out of water. And then it's got a bigger problem: it can't breathe.

Peter K. Fallon is a similar kind of fish, leaping in and out of the water all around us, and writing up the results of his mid-air observations. And you may already know that the image of a fish out of water is actually an ancient symbol of wisdom, or enlightenment, or what we would nowadays call "consciousness-raising." According to an author writing with authority in ISBN-13: 978-0877288503, on page 32, "in ancient Chinese art fish are sometimes depicted jumping out of the 'water gate,' freeing themselves from the psychic realm, to enter the world of the spirit." The fish pictured this way in Chinese paintings are normally carp, but don't go there, because they have different connotations in the East than they do in the West.

If you read the essays collected herein, even some of them, you will have committed the cultural heresy of the title. You will have committed the act of contemplation, in defiance of the noise, rush, bright colors, and distraction from the unmitigated disaster of technological society's clustercuss all around you. And that will be a deviant thing to do.

Come on in: the water is fine.

> Read Mercer Schuchardt
> Wheaton, Illinois, USA,
> Tuesday, November 27, 2012.

Endnotes

1. *Foreword*   Robert Louis Stevenson, *Virginibus Puerisque*, 1881.

2. Jacques Ellul, *Sources and Trajectories: Eight Early Articles by Jacques Ellul that Set the Stage*, Ed. Marva J. Dawn (Grand Rapids, MI: Eerdman's Publishing, 1997), p. 40.

Contemplation as Defiance/Deviance

In his *Nicomachean Ethics*, Aristotle correctly identified happiness as the end of all human action. But Aristotle also noted – correctly – that different people define happiness in different ways. Careful readers of Aristotle will notice the subtle defiance, not in his tone, which is ever reasoned and devoid of passion, but in his unwavering insistence that what most people define as happiness is really something else; something temporary, something contingent on circumstances. It may be pleasure, it may be honor, it may be health or prosperity or the esteem of others. It could be nothing more than a gratification of the senses, whether crude or highly refined: the scratching of an itch, the experience of a work of art, the filling of an empty belly, the momentary loss of self in the passionate embrace of another.

These are goods, to be sure; but they are not *the* good. They are but instrumental goods, means to some other end which is itself only the means to another, and so on. But one thing and one thing only is final and self-sufficient; one thing is permanent and independent of circumstances or other more temporary ends. *That* is happiness. And happiness, Aristotle assures us with a certainty that my students identify as arrogance, is an activity of the soul in conformity with human virtue, and the quintessential human virtue is *reason*. For Aristotle, the life spent in contemplation is the end of all human action. Contemplation empowers happiness.

None of this, I am forced to say at the outset, is my argument in this essay. Even if I agreed with these statements (and I am certainly sympathetic to them) I know enough to realize what a "hard sell" they must be in a highly technologically developed society such as ours; not only to our students, but to many of our faculty colleagues, to many reading this book right now, and to most if not all (I would venture to say) academic administrators.

The argument for the profound importance of contemplation to the human soul will sound, well, odd to the 21st century student who, if nothing else, is wrapped up in the utilitarian mindset of a culture that values its technological *means* far more than *any given end.* Indeed, as Jacques Ellul has argued, we live in a world of proliferating means that threaten to replace ends entirely (or, perhaps, already have). We do things, more and more, simply because we *can*, and certainly not because we have questioned the ethical implications of our actions which, of course, appear perfectly normal to us.

There is, then, an ethical dimension to contemplation after all which ought to result in an ethical attention to our activity. I believe this is an appropriate interpretation of Thomas Aquinas' exhortation, "To contemplate and to give to others the fruits of contemplation." The problem is, for many people, and especially for today's students, even *seeing* in the first place this ethical imperative to action based in, and flowing from, an inner search for meaning. In a culture that emphasizes external experience, a culture that emphasizes engagement through the senses, a culture that floods our senses with a superabundance of information through a multiplicity of channels, a culture that leaves us little time – if any – for quiet introspection, how do we even begin to approach contemplation, let alone share its fruit with others?

Are our students, however, really challenged in creating a contemplative life? I argue that yes, they are, and offer these statistics. According to the Kaiser Family Foundation's 2003 study *Zero to Six: Electronic Media in the Lives of Infants, Toddlers, and Preschoolers*, nearly all children (99%) live in a home with a TV set, half (50%) have three or more TVs, and one-third (36%) have a TV in their bedroom. Almost three out of four (73%) have a computer at home, and about half (49%) have at least one video game player.[1] Virtually half (48%) of all children six and under use a computer on a daily basis, and nearly a third (30%) regularly play video games.[2] Children six and under spend an average of about two hours a day with screen media (1:58), three times as much time as they spend reading or being read to (39 minutes). Thirty-six percent of all children six and under have their own TV in their bedroom (30% of zero- to three-year-olds and 43% of four to six-year-olds); more than a quarter (27%) have their own VCR or DVD player, and one in ten (10%) has his/her own video game console in the bedroom room.[3] It is no surprise, then, to learn that in their 2011 study *Generation M2: Media in the lives of 8- to 18-Year-Olds*, the Kaiser Foundation found that young people today pack a total of 10 hours and 45 minutes worth of mediated interaction with the world into 7½ multi-tasked hours each day – an increase of almost 2¼ hours since their previous survey in 2006.[4]

Many of us today, of course, are not inclined to see any of this as a problem.

It is a truism today, in this highly technologically-developed culture, that students need technical computer skills. Equally truistic (and, not incidentally, true) is that the workplace has become highly technological. Even more truistic – and far more disturbing – are the shifts in education over the last two decades as public elementary schools, public and private high schools, and colleges and universities have invested scores of billions of dollars on "digital infrastructure," computers, monitors and printers, "smart classrooms," all to "meet the demands" of this new technological workplace.

We won't dwell on the fact – an inconvenient truth? – that those technological investments have coincided with a decline in American reading behaviors, in reading and reading comprehension scores, in overall academic achievement, in the phenomenon – all too familiar to us in academia – of "grade inflation," in an alarming collapse of our students' understanding of their own history (to say nothing of the history of the rest of the world), rising ignorance of world and American geography, with an abandonment of the idea of objectivity, and with an increasingly subjective, even solipsistic, emphasis on *personal* experience. Ignore all this. Or, if we find it impossible to ignore, then let's blame the teachers.

It is enough, for my purposes at least, to observe how completely and unquestioningly we have accepted the technological narrative and how quickly we have assimilated its values. If my characterizations of technology's actual cultural effects – and our blindness to them – sound defiant to your ears, and especially if they sound deviant, then I believe I've made my point about our quickness to accept and assimilate.

Deviant?

It occurred to me while writing this essay (long after its conception and submission) that by changing one letter of its title a powerful parallel argument emerges, and it is that contemplation is itself not only essentially an act of defiance, but also of deviance. Let me explain myself.

Defiance is a political act, whether on the level of society or of interpersonal interaction, and is judged objectively. Defiance implies the willful breaking of formal conventional rules. A defiant act is a willful rebellion against some social institution, whether it is the state, the church, the school, or the family. It is an implicitly political statement that says "I will not cooperate with something I don't like." A defiant person *chooses* to be defiant.

Deviance is another story entirely, a moral issue. To be deviant is to be different – almost ontologically so – from others. A deviant act is no deliberate rebellion against a social institution, but an innate response to a socially-constructed reality. Deviance is always judged subjectively according to culturally-defined norms, created over time by convention and based on widely (but not universally) shared values. These values become the "unquestionable truths" of a culture. A deviant may appear, to those in the mainstream, as someone who is defiant; that the deviation from the norm is willful and chosen specifically to flout the accepted cultural conventions, rather than the authentic expression of an individual's personal experience. But more than mere defiance (which, after all, deals with externalities), deviance appears subversive; an utter lack of respect for the sacred, for the values of one's peers, one's society. It appears to mainstream culture a sign of moral malformation. No deviant *chooses* to be different.

I stand here today to confess – no, to profess! – both my defiance and my deviance, as well as my desire, in my life as a Dominican educator, to inspire my students in similar acts of defiance and deviance. The contemplative person in today's world *must* stand out as both a rebel and a misfit. It could hardly be otherwise, for we have constructed for ourselves a world where the senses are ascendant and the interior life unbearable.

In both his 1962 sociological treatise *The Technological Society* and his seminal 1948 theological work *The Presence of the Kingdom* Jacques Ellul wrote of the proliferation of technique – which includes both machines and the new methods of social, political, and cultural organization they make necessary – and the parallel disappearance of human ends.

What I referred to a few minutes ago as *the technological narrative* is the value system of the technological society. Our entire information infrastructure and all of its constituent parts – the various media of communication, but also our schools, our government, our houses of worship, our workplaces, and even our families – function to transmit and perpetuate the fundamental values of technique: efficiency, speed, productivity, new-ness, profit, ease, convenience, uniformity, consumption, "progress," etc. "Happiness" loses all connection with the idea of finality and non-contingency and becomes commoditized, a thing to be marketed, bought, and enjoyed. The technological society prospers more through temporary, contingent ends. Technique, consequently, exists not only as the production method, but also as the product. All human behavior is rationalized by – and judged within the context of – technique. Technique in all the senses of the word is, consequently, the new god of the technological society, our *ultimate concern* to use Paul Tillich's phrase. The machine – whether powered by coal and steam, fossil fuels and internal combustion, or nuclear fission; whether mechanical or electro-mechanical or electronic or digital – is the incarnation of technique in our midst. And the values of technique, the "spirit" of technique – greater efficiency, the extension of our senses, the expansion of our power, increasing productivity, providing convenience, amusement, and distraction – these are the third person of this particular trinity (I stop just short of calling it an *unholy trinity* to maintain at least a semblance of empiric objectivity).

In the technological society, it is no longer necessary that our actions be oriented to, or explained by, any particular end. The iPad is a closed, self-justifying argument for itself, predicated on the unquestioned – and, in my opinion, spurious – assumption that information that I can get quickly without leaving my chair is better than information I need to leave the house for. And this speed and convenience in the movement of information, I feel obliged to point out, comes at an invisible cost felt not by those living in the technological society, but in the less technologically developed world: ecological catastrophe and damage to health (in the mining of heavy metals), labor exploitation, and growing economic inequality. Is there an app for that?

Many of us, however, reassure ourselves that our technologies are after all merely means to some desired end. We tell ourselves that our computers, or some social network, or a television series, or our smart phones, or our mp3 players make our lives more pleasant, easier; make our work more productive; give us greater leisure time; make us happy; all messages consistent with the technological narrative. I will not dwell on what I hope is the obviousness of the irony here. I will not dwell on the fact that we are working harder and longer than ever before, we seem to have less rather than more leisure time (and what time we have we tend to fill with technological diversions), and live lives of stress and anxiety rather than happiness. I will only remind you that Aristotle would say these "ends" we have persuaded ourselves that we are seeking are all contingent and not final ends, and that Aquinas might say that these "actions" are the fruit *not* of contemplation, but of its avoidance. Or, to paraphrase Henry David Thoreau, our inventions are just pretty toys, which distract our attention from serious things. They are but improved means to an unimproved end.

There is one more point I need to make that is far more significant than my allusion to the distractions of materialism and technique. The phenomena I have been describing to you up until now have all been behavioral ones. They result from our *choices*, choices I contend are poorly made on the basis of faulty values, the values of the technological society. While new choices could be easily made based on (what I believe to be) more worthy values, I don't expect many listening today to agree with me simply on the strength of my *formidable* powers of persuasion. Hardly. Indeed, I expect many will find my attitude stuffy, old-fashioned, defiant and more than a little bit deviant.

But beyond the behavioral, there are biological factors that similarly demand our defiance of cultural norms. A growing body of neurological research supports my contention that human beings, formed in the crucible of a sensory-based and imagistic technological culture, will soon be entirely incapable of contemplation – at least in any sense that we have used the word before. Studies made possible by the development of new measurement instruments – not only electroencephalography, CAT and PET scans, but MRIs, fMRIs (functional magnetic resonance imaging) and other new tools – allow researchers to measure brain activity and to view the firings across synaptic pathways characteristic of different types of cognitive activities. These studies confirm what many communication scholars – particularly those who study language and literacy – have theorized about for decades: that there are not only specific areas in the brain, but specific neural pathways that are dedicated to reading, as well as to the profoundly contemplative state one experiences when engaged in the deep reading of a text. Indeed, deep reading and deep thought activate nearly identical synaptic pathways across identical areas of the brain, with the possible (but not necessary) exception of the visual cortex.

Furthermore, there is a threshold for learning – not in the cognitive or behavioral senses, but in the neurological one: the "programming" or mapping of neural pathways for different activities that will demand one type of activity will dominate others in a person's life. The limits of cerebral plasticity necessitate that, if a child is to be a reader (that is to say, one with the ability to linger over and think deeply about a text, its meaning, its consequences), that child must engage in the cognitive experiences that activate the necessary and proper synaptic pathways as early and often as possible, and avoid those experiences – like television, video games, and other screen media – that activate competing pathways.

Simply put, the child growing in an environment of external images, images not of her own making, over which she has no control but to watch and react, will not develop the neural pathways necessary to make her anything other than an uncomfortable, casual reader, and will find deep, sustained, conceptual thought difficult. And this is *exactly* the opposite of the environment we have created for our children to develop within. For those interested, I have prepared a brief bibliography of books and studies that support these claims.

In order to address these problems, I have used a number of strategies over the last two decades that aim at helping students become aware of the extent of their engagement with mediated realities. The *Personal Media Inventory* demands students keep track of all mediated experiences – including multi-mediation – by category for the space of a week. Never a student's favorite assignment, the Personal Media Inventory is always a learning experience, and frequently a painful one. I've been assigning this exercise since 1993 and the responses from students have always fallen into two categories. There are first the defensive or denying responses (and here I quote from actual student responses from the most recent spring semester):

I know my hours are high mostly because of my job where multiple media are running at the same time. I just got the internet at home this semester because I had to take 3 out of my 6 classes online. I don't use any social networking media nor do I really talk or text on an hourly basis on my off or down time. Most of it is at work to learn, demonstrate, and hopefully sell devices for the use of technology for voice and/or data.

And this one:

I have the television on a lot at home (about six hours each day) but I'm not really watching it. It's more like background noise. Every once in a while something comes on that catches my attention but most of the time I'm not paying attention at all. I don't play violent video games because I think they glorify violence, but do enjoy Flock and Peggle (about an hour each day).

The other type of response is what I call the embarrassed or apologetic response, as though the student feels as though he or she has been caught in a shameful act (and again these are actual student comments):

The results of my Personal Media Inventory are more alarming than expected. I am on the computer so incredibly much. More than I would have thought. An additional observation is that I spend an equal amount of time indulging in other sorts of media, equally alarming as well. It is hard to imagine a world without this.

And this one:

I was surprised at the amount of the day I spend interacting with media. It doesn't seem like a lot when I am actually doing it, but writing it all down like this makes me feel like it would be hard to go a day completely without it. For someone who loves being outside and away from technology, I sure do spend a lot of time with it. It really makes me want to pay attention to what I am doing and start involving myself less with media.

Media Journals are descriptive narratives of students' meaning-making processes while engaging mediated realities. Non-mandatory – but strongly encouraged – ***Media Fasts*** or

Media Diets encourage students to give in-class reports of their personal reactions (many students describe the experience as akin to quitting smoking). These strategies – and others that I use – frequently fall flat; the powerful hold of the mediated experience on minds shaped in a mediated culture is impressive. But some of my students over the years have decreased their dependence on image-based media, or have shifted to media (or, at least, reported to me that they have done so) that allow for and even model contemplative thought (e.g., books, as opposed to TV, video games, or Internet), and have found time – and space – to contemplate (and look more critically at) their culture. Some students who have chosen to do so have described a sense of relief or even "liberation," and one student went so far as to call it "an act of defiance" against a culture of mass-produced realities. The fruits of these students' actions *must* be affected by such a defiant self-liberation. It is, at any rate, my most fervent hope.

I'm about finished with my argument. I won't fool myself into thinking you'll all close this book or move on to the next chapter and, on the strength of one person's rhetoric, rethink your pedagogy – or your strategic plans – and banish Powerpoint and YouTube and iPads from your classrooms. I would be happy that I have accomplished something if a handful of you – even one other person – is intrigued enough to take a copy of the bibliography, to read the studies I've listed, to consider the evidence they present, and to think – long, hard, and deeply – about just how smart a "smart classroom" really is. I'm fully aware the extent to which my argument defies conventional wisdom and deviates from the current pedagogical norm. But if we, educators – Dominican or otherwise – can't or won't raise these objections, can't question the received "wisdom" of our technological culture; if we can't or won't break the spell of glib magicians who have persuaded us that the emperor – naked in the eyes of both man and God – is clad in royal raiment that only the ignorant – or deviant – can't see, then I wonder who can? If we, my fellow Dominican and lay educators, parents, colleagues, and students, rather than fighting heresies

– admittedly comforting and popular ones – embrace them and *teach* them, the consequences of our actions may be too dire to contemplate.

Brief Bibliography

Popular Books:

Changeux, J.P. *The Physiology of Truth: Neuroscience and Human Knowledge.* Cambridge, MA: The Belknap Press, 2004.

Dehaene, Stanislas, *Reading in the Brain: The Science and Evolution of a Human Invention.* New York: Viking, 2009.

Fallon, Peter K., *The Metaphysics of Media: Toward an End to Postmodern Cynicism and the Construction of a Virtuous Reality.* Scranton, PA: The University of Scranton Press, 2010.

Wolf, Maryanne, *Proust and the Squid: The Story and Science of the Reading Brain.* New York: HarperCollins, 2007.

Published Research:

Aghababian, V., and Nazir, T.A. *Developing Normal Reading Skills: Aspects of the Visual Processes Underlying Word Recognition* in Journal of Experimental Child Psychology 76(2):123-150.

Anderson, Daniel R., Fite, Katherine V., Petrovich, Nicole, and Hirsch, Joy. *Cortical Activation While Watching Video Montage: An fMRI Study* in Media Psychology, 2006, Vol. 8, No. 1.

Bavelier, D., Corina, D., Jezzard, P., Padmanabhan, S., Clark, V. P., Karni, A., Prinster, A., Braun, A., Lalwani, A., Rauschecker, J. P., Turner R., and Neville, H. *"Sentence Reading: A Functional MRI Study at 4 Tesla"* in The Journal of Cognitive Neuroscience, Vol 9.

Beaulieu, C., Plewes, C., Paulson, L.A., Roy, D., Snook, L., Concha, L., and Phillips, L. *Imaging Brain Connectivity in Children With Diverse Reading Ability* in Neuroimage 25(4):1266-1271.

Bentin, S., Mouchetant-Rostaing, Y., Giard, M.H., Echallier, J.F., and
Pernier, J. *ERP Manifestations of Processing Printed Words at
Different Psycholinguistic Levels: Time Course and Scalp Dis-
tribution* in Journal of Cognitive Neuroscience 11:235-260.

Cheour, M., Ceponiene, R., Lehtokoske, A., Luuk, A., Allik, J., Alho,
K., and Naatanen, R. *Development of Language-specific Pho-
neme Representations in the Infant Brain* in Nature Neuroscience 1(5):351-353.

Cohen, L., and Dehaene, S., *Specialization Within the Ventral
Stream: The Case for the Visual Word Form Area* in Neuroimage
22(1):466-476.

Dehaene, S., *Electrophysiological Evidence for Category-specific
Word Processing in the Normal Human Brain* in NeuroReport
6:2153-2157.

Fiez, J.A., and Petersen, S.E., *Neuroimaging Studies of Word Reading*
in Proceedings of the National Academy of Sciences 95(3):914-
921.

Gaillard, W.D., Balsamo, L.M., Ibrahim, Z., Sachs, B.C., and Xu, B.
*fMRI Identifies Regional Specialization of Neural Networks for
Reading in Young Children* in Neurology 60(1):94-100.

McCandliss, B.D., Cohen, L., and Dehaene, S. *The Visual Word Form
Area:Expertise for Reading in the Fusiform Gyrus* in Trends in
Cognitive Sciences 7:293-299.

ENDNOTES

1. Rideout, Victoria J., et al., *Zero to Six: Electronic Media in
the Lives of Infants, Toddlers, and Pre-Schoolers* (Henry J. Kaiser
Family Foundation, 2003), p. 4.

2. Ibid.

3. Ibid., p. 7.

4. Rideout, Victoria J., et al., *Generation M2: Media in the lives
of 8- to 18-Year-Olds* (Henry J. Kaiser Family Foundation, 2011),
p. 3.

The Occupy Movement and Catholic Social Justice [i]

My father used to say, "Anything worth doing is worth overdoing." I suspect a few people will think I'm overdoing it, that I'm jumping the gun, that I'm trying to close down discussion of an issue before it even gets started with a peremptory challenge. I am indeed going to begin my few minutes with you tonight by unfairly challenging Thomas McNamara's theme, "Capitalism as the Solution, Not the Problem" before he even gets a chance to present it to us. This provocative title raised my eyebrows when I read it a week ago, and my imagination, I have to admit, ran a little wild. Perhaps, I thought, the title was meant to be ironic, or to throw us off the track while he presents an argument that does, after all, assign fair responsibility to our economic system – and those who administer it – for our current woes. We'll all know, in a matter of minutes, when we hear Mr. McNamara speak, whether I'm overdoing it or not. In the meantime, some thoughts.

To propose that Capitalism is the solution to our current

On November 16, 2011 (the day after NYC cops in riot gear evicted a peaceful protest in Zuccotti Park) I took part in a panel at Molloy College in Rockville Centre, NY, on Occupy Wall Street and the Occupy movement. The panel was sponsored by Molloy's Center for Social and Ethical Concerns (CSEC) and hosted by Molloy's VP for Advancement Ed Thompson. I was joined on the panel by Dr. Michael Russo, Professor of Philosophy and Director of CSEC, and Thomas J. MacNamara, adjunct Instructor in Molloy's Business program and Partner-in-Charge of the Litigation Practice Group at Certilman Balin Adler & Hyman, LLP. This essay is a slightly revised version of my presentation.

economic problems, as I expect Mr. McNamara to do in a few minutes, is certainly reasonable, and it is a proposition with which I whole-heartedly concur. However, to propose in the same sentence that Capitalism is not at the same time *the very cause* of our current economic problems is, I believe, an exercise in sophistry. The equation is incomplete, important variables are missing. What does Mr. McNamara mean by "Capitalism"? What kind of Capitalism is a solution to the problems we're facing right now in the United States and the world? For there is no single thing that exists objectively somewhere out there in the universe known as "Capitalism." There is no perfect "Capitalism" dwelling in some realm of perfection – like Plato's realm of ideal forms – of which our "Capitalism" is merely an imperfect shadow. Capitalism is a game we play, a game created by humans and whose rules are invented – and reinvented constantly – by humans. And if we can see this to be the actual state of affairs, we can perhaps recognize that the rules by which we've been playing the game for several decades now are quite unfair, unjust, and unhealthy. The "Capitalism" described by Adam Smith in his treatise of 1776, *An Inquiry into the Nature and Causes of the Wealth of Nations*, is not the "Capitalism" we have seen played out before us over the last thirty or forty or fifty years. Smith's description of a free-market balancing forces of supply and demand, production and labor, founded on (and here's an important word) *enlightened* self-interest and intended to serve human *needs* (another incredibly important word) bears very little resemblance to a system that seems motivated by the quest for profit to the detriment of labor, the outsourcing of production to other countries, and the creation of artificial, mass-manufactured "needs," needs that are not at all "enlightened" in any sense of the word, but entirely irrational and emotional.

And here's the thing: we should have known that this was the case a long time ago. Worse, I suspect we've always known and simply chose to ignore it because we were all pretty comfortable, well-fed, and surrounded by the diversions and amusements of our mass-mediated culture. Worse still: we who call ourselves Catholics and Christians have a greater obligation to recognize and act on these things than others who have not heard the good news of Christ. We have been warned of the inevitability of economic injustice and economic injury and we have ignored those warnings. Like my namesake Peter, we have had ample opportunity to embrace Christ and the suffering that that embrace entails, and we have denied Him.

As early as 1891 Pope Leo XIII in his encyclical *Rerum Novarum* warned us in words remarkable for their 21st century familiarity that "it has come to pass that working men have been surrendered, isolated and helpless, to the hardheartedness of employers and the greed of unchecked competition. The mischief has been increased by rapacious usury, which, although more than once condemned by the Church, is nevertheless, under a different guise, but with like injustice, still practiced by covetous and grasping men. To this must be added that the hiring of labor and the conduct of trade are concentrated in the hands of comparatively few; so that a small number of very rich men have been able to lay upon the teeming masses of the laboring poor a yoke little better than that of slavery itself."[1]

In 1891 the problems with Capitalism were already apparent to the Church: greed on the part of the owners and controllers of the means of production; unjust working and living conditions for workers. But this was before the age of widespread electronic media, before the age of a greater awareness of the world, even on the part of the Holy Father, before the age of awareness of the ecological nature of human relationships. By the middle of the 20th century, however, a new age had truly arisen and the Church was paying attention.

In 1961, John XXIII wrote in his encyclical *Mater et Magistra* that human labor must not be regarded merely as a commodity but as a distinctly human activity deserving of respect for its intrinsic dignity. As a result of this inherent human dignity, and because for many "man's work is his sole means of livelihood," its remuneration "cannot be made to depend on the state of the market. It must be determined by the laws of justice and equity."[2] Private ownership of property, the Holy Father told us, was a natural right inalienable by any political power. But, he explained, "it naturally entails a social obligation as well. It is a right which must be exercised not only for one's own personal benefit but also for the benefit of others."[3]

In his 1967 encyclical *Populorum Progressio* Pope Paul VI warned us flatly that "No one may appropriate surplus goods solely for his own private use when others lack the bare necessities of life... the right of private property may never be exercised to the detriment of the common good."[4]

By 1987 the encyclicals dealing with social justice issues had a distinctly political tone – not political in a partisan sense, but in the sense that it was the Church's clear stand that both the political state and the economic structure of that state were constructed to serve the needs of people, and not the other way around. One of the most stunning statements I've heard from my Church came in that year of 1987 in Pope John Paul II's *Solicitudo Rei Socialis* (On Social Matters). "On Social Matters" is a brilliant critique of global economics at the end of the 20th century – at the cusp of the "New World Order" that would make itself known to the world in a few short years. It is a courageous stand for and defense of Christian principles in the face of *both* Soviet collectivism and unregulated, expansionist, laissez faire Capitalism.

John Paul looked at the history of human development in the twentieth century – and particularly of the post-war period – and found that the proliferation of injustice and poverty had been just as common (if not more so) than the proliferation of equality and prosperity.[5] He denounced the "automatic" – that is to say unregulated – functioning of economic policies that benefitted the wealthy investor over the laborer sliding, day by day, ever more deeply into poverty.[6] He denounced the failure (or refusal) of developed countries to forgive the debt of developing countries, most of whom had entailed this debt in the first place during the arduous process of removing themselves from the yoke of colonialism by the developed countries of the west.[7] And he denounced – although I'd be willing to bet my last dollar that there is no one in this audience this evening who is aware of this – unregulated, global, laissez faire, (so-called) "free-market" Capitalism as being morally equivalent to Communism in the "structures of sin" with which each presents the worker. Communism is dead, and rightly so, for among its other sins it denied the essential dignity and liberty of the human soul. But something we're still calling "Capitalism" lives on, and it is instructive to read John Paul's descriptions of the various structures of sin that Capitalism – unregulated by reason and good will – presents to us.[8] I'll list just a few: 1] the all-consuming desire for profit; 2] the thirst for power, with the intention of imposing one's will upon others; 3] idolatry of money, ideology, class, technology; 4] the abuse of resources as though they were inexhaustible and the amassing of resources by the wealthy at the expense of the poor.[9]

I have spent several minutes thus far making reference to several Papal encyclicals and you kind folks in the audience may be thinking at this moment, *what in the world does this have to do with a movement made up of unwashed, drug-crazed, over-sexed, hippy anarchists?* Well, if you phrased your question in this way there's nothing I can say to persuade you that the Occupy Movement has *anything* to do with Catholic social teaching. But I still have a few minutes left and I'm going to try to explain my point.

First, I'd call your attention to several of the works of the late French sociologist, media critic and Christian theologian Jacques Ellul, especially his works *The Technological Society, Propaganda: The Formation of Men's Attitudes,* and *The Presence of the Kingdom.* The technological society, Ellul tells us, is predicated on a number of values that supersede all other values: efficiency, productivity, profit, speed, convenience, and consumption, among others. These values express themselves in myth: social narratives that rationalize our attitudes, beliefs, and behaviors. To seek efficiency – and even better, to achieve it – comes to be seen as an objective good. To be productive is an objective good. To make a profit, to provide convenience, to consume – all these things constitute the value system of the technological society. They are assimilated into the culture of technologically developed societies, and assimilated by individuals at an early age. They suffuse our information environment and become self-fulfilling and self-sustaining prophecies. Our advertisements – but also our news, sports, and entertainment programming – are constant reinforcements of the values of the technological society. This "total propaganda" (in Ellul's words) makes use of all the available media of communication at all times and creates a closed system of information that is not only inescapable, but which we, its targets, actually come to crave. Material consumption becomes the raison d'etre of technological man, and when we are brutally attacked by evil-doers we don't blink an eye when our President urges us to show the terrorists they have not won by going shopping.[10]

The values of technology, as I said, become self-justifying and self-fulfilling and human culture takes on, under the influence of highly-developed technology, a characteristic that never existed before the twentieth century: the loss of the end. With the proliferation of technological means, human beings have lost all sight of the end of action. To what end do we do the things we do in our lives? Ellul tells us that we no longer see the satisfaction of human needs as the end of human action. We do things simply because our technologies make things possible. We consume things simply because we can. We use things simply because we can. To what end was the iPad created? Wait – better question: to what end does *anyone* watch "Jersey Shore"?

Our lives are increasingly mediated and our attentions are increasingly focused on ourselves, and that's the way we want it. "The dramatic characteristic of this epoch," Ellul tells us, "in this sphere, is that man no longer grasps anything but shadows. He believes in these shadows, he lives in them, and dies for them. Reality disappears, the reality of man for himself, and the reality of the facts which surround him."[11] It's the end of the world as we know it, and I feel fine.

But Ellul also tells us that there are certain objective conditions for the existence of total propaganda, and the loss of one or more of these conditions weakens the overall effectiveness of propaganda. These conditions include the enjoyment of general prosperity, the enjoyment of a general level of education, and a shared vision of reality based on shared information. It is ironic, then, that the problems of unregulated Capitalism have resulted in growing poverty, a falling standard of living, a failure of education to create a common culture imbued with common knowledge, and an increasingly polarized marketplace of ideas. To put it simply, the Occupy Movement became inevitable as soon as enough people stopped believing that they were sharing in the benefits promised by the values of the technological society: efficiency, productivity, profit, speed, convenience, and consumption. For some people, this was some time ago. We should all be alarmed at what this movement actually represents: the large-scale and widespread failure of the game of Capitalism – according to the rules by which we are currently playing it. And *that* is the problem. So how can Capitalism possibly be its own solution?

The answer is really quite simple – once we reject the ideology of the technological society and actually go back to some fundamental sources: Adam Smith, the Enlightenment social philosophers, non-ideological economists, Sacred Scripture, and the teaching authority of the Holy Father. Capitalism needs some new rules – or, in fact more accurately – we need to go back to playing the game of Capitalism by older rules. We need to reclaim human ends in Capitalism. Profit is good. But profit can't be the end of a just economic system. A just economic system serves human needs. Globalization – the organized spread of Capitalism through direct foreign investment via WTO, IMF, and the World Bank – has resulted in an increase in wealth around the world, to be sure. But it has also resulted in an increase in poverty and a growing income gap – globally and within nations – between the richest and the poorest. In both numbers and percentages, poverty has continued to grow globally in the last forty years.[12]

We need regulation. As Paul VI told us as far back as 1967, when "private gain and basic community needs conflict with one another," it is for the public authorities "to seek a solution to these questions, with the active involvement of individual citizens and social groups." The recent report of the Pontifical Council for Justice and Peace noted that our current economic crisis was created in no small part by "an economic liberalism that spurns rules and controls."[13] Whose conception of "economic liberalism" is referred to in this report? Well, certainly free-market economists, CEOs, Boards of Directors and their stockholders, and – to the extent that we accept the idea that corporations are "persons" – we'd have to say corporations themselves. But it is also *our* conception of what constitutes Capitalism. And we'll have to get over it. As the Pontifical Council advises, what is needed is "a spirit of solidarity" among all constituent parts of the economy "that transcends personal utility for the good of the community."

To borrow Jacques Ellul's terms, we have found that all the things that our culture has sold us over the last several decades as being "new" and "revolutionary" were rather tired and recycled ideas that failed in the past, even if they provided some few people with power and wealth. What we need, Ellul said, is a "revolutionary Christianity," which rejects ideologies of the left or of the right, which is non-partisan even as it is profoundly political, and which is based not on institutional principles, but on the Gospel message: "Love God with your whole heart, mind, soul, and body; and love your neighbor as you love yourself." To this end we need to reclaim the satisfaction of human needs as the end of all activity, rebuild distinctly human interpersonal relationships, rediscover our own human power and sovereignty (as opposed to the illusions of power and sovereignty provided by technologies and material consumables), and regain faith in the worth of the *common good*. If we can do this, we will be more in conformity with Catholic social justice teaching. And, perhaps to our surprise, we will be in conformity with much of the message of the Occupy Movement.

My father was a funny guy – but wise beyond peoples' expectations. He left me with a wealth of sayings and I quote him extensively when I speak publicly. There's one more I'd like to share. My Dad always said: "It's not what you say or what you look like or who your friends are, but *what you do* that makes you the person you are." And I'll leave it at that

ENDNOTES

1. Leo XIII, Encyclical Rerum Novarum (May 15, 1891): Leonis XIII P. M. Acta, XI, Romae 1892. Accessed November 14, 2011 from: http://www.vatican.va/holy_father/leo_xiii/encyclicals/documents/ hf_l-xiii_enc_15051891_rerum-novarum_en.html

2. John XXIII, Mater et Magistra (May 15, 1961); AAS 53 (1961). Accessed November 14, 2011 from: http://www.vatican.va/holy_ father/john_xxiii/encyclicals/documents/hf_j-xxiii_enc_15051961_ mater_en.html

3. Ibid.

4. Paul VI, Populorum Progressio (March 26, 1967). Accessed November 14, 2011 from: http://www.vatican.va/holy_father/ paul_vi/encyclicals/documents/hf_p-vi_enc_26031967_populorum_ en.html

5. Ioannes Paulus PP. II, Sollicitudo rei socialis (December 30,1987), part three. Accessed November 3, 2011 from: http://www. vatican.va/edocs/ENG0223/__P4.HTM

6. Ibid.

7. Ibid., part six. http://www.vatican.va/edocs/ENG0223/__ P7.HTM

8. Ibid., part five. http://www.vatican.va/edocs/ENG0223/__ P6.HTM

9. Ibid.,

10. Vardie, Jill and Chris Wattie, "Shopping is Patriotic, Leaders Say," National Post (Canada), September 28, 2001. Accessed June 3, 2006 from: http://commondreams.org/headlines01/0929-04.htm

11 Jacques Ellul, *The Presence of the Kingdom* (Colorado Springs: Helmers and Howard, 1989), p. 82.

12.   Agence France-Presse, "Global Poverty Doubled Since 1970s: UN," November 25, 2010. Accessed on November 14, 2011 from:http://www.rawstory.com/rs/2010/11/25/global-poverty-doubled-1970s/ See also: World Bank, "Poverty in an Age of Globalization," October 2000. Accessed June 17, 2007 from: http://econ.la.psu.edu/~bickes/povglobal.pdf

13. Pontifical Council for Justice and Peace, "Toward Reforming the International Financial and Monetary Systems in the Context of Global Public Authority," October 24, 2011. Accessed on October 25, 2011 from: http://www.news.va/en/news/full-text-note-on-financial-reform-from-the-pontif

In the Dark:
Why Ignorance Survives in an
Age of Information

"What we don't know won't hurt us...." This old saying begs a
burning question about democracy, mass communication, and
the free-market capitalist view of information as commodity.
It is a question with both an ethical and a moral dimension
and it has been resisted in the past by the empirical objectivity
of academia wherein values based on unchanging truths are
always suspect. I propose that, in a time of war, in the face
of growing global anti-Americanism, it is time to face this
question without flinching.

The old joke begins, "I have some good news and some
bad news...." Well, I have some good news and some bad
news for us all. First the good news about ignorance, defined
in the Catholic Encyclopedia as a "lack of knowledge about
a thing in a being capable of knowing."[1] The good news is
that ignorance "is said to be invincible when it cannot be
dispelled by the reasonable diligence a prudent (person) would
be expected to exercise in a given situation,"[2] that is, when
we've done everything we can, morally and ethically speaking,
to learn the truth. Invincible ignorance is always a valid excuse
and excludes us, in the theological sense, from sin because
the agent "is inculpably unaware of the nature of a situation
or the obligations it involves."[3] Now the bad news: we may
be in trouble (again, theologically, in "a state of sin") if we
allow the existence of evil *even when we are ignorant of it*,
if that ignorance is vincible, "that which could be dispelled
by the application of reasonable diligence,"[4] in a word, the

diligence a sensible and prudent person would use under the circumstances.

A sad fact I'd like to share with you about this essay is that there's nothing new in it. It represents no new theory, no new data, no new ideas. It is rather a synthesis of ideas, data, and theories that have been at our fingertips for years. My thesis is simply this: that with all the information at our disposal, with all the vast resources of mass communication technologies available to us, we are ignorant of our world and happy and complacent in our ignorance. We are guilty of an ignorance easily dispelled — a supremely vincible ignorance — and if this is so we ought to be ashamed. This is the bad news to which I refer. A popular television show of recent years has told us week after week "the truth is out there..." The truth *is* out there, and the extent to which we don't see it, or won't see it, is a measure of our human imperfection. To live in a world where we don't have to see the ugly realities of life is to live in a world of fantasy. Such a fantasy world may make us feel more secure, more comfortable, but it does nothing to help anyone in the *real* world. And, in truth, it's not helping us, either; it's killing us.

But are we really ignorant? And if so are we really to blame? In a mass culture such as ours, we depend on our electronic media of mass communication to be our eyes and ears, our "window on the world." More than that (as Marshall McLuhan liked to point out) the network of transoceanic and transcontinental cables and the vast system of satellites floating miles above the earth, linking the world together through radio, television, telephone, and computers can function as a sort of global central nervous system, moving all of humanity closer and closer to becoming a single global organism.

But I suggest that our eyes and ears are closed, and deliberately so, consciously so. I suggest that for all the millions and billions of dollars spent every year on expanding the communication potential of the human species, for all of the hundreds of channels of broadcast and cable programming, for the hundreds of thousands of radio outlets worldwide, for the amazing rise of cellular technology, for all that it appears that human beings are more closely linked to each other and to the world than ever before, we in fact learn and know very little of the world, and have used our communication technologies — deliberately — to cut ourselves off from it. We *"walk in the darkness, and do not know where we are going because the darkness has blinded our eyes."*[5]

How can this be? We live, after all, in the much-vaunted "information age," an age where we seem — by all appearances — to be in tune with all that is going on around us. We are "all connected" — or so the old phone company advertisement told us. We wake every morning to a litany of disasters, scandals, crimes, and controversies. We know what the weather will be like for the next five days in NY, Chicago and Phoenix. We know whether our stocks have made or lost money in the last two hours, and whether our favorite ball team won last night. We believe that we have more information at our fingertips than any people in the history of humankind have had at their disposable, and we're right. And we believe we have enough information to make responsible, ethical choices in our lives, and we're wrong.

So much of what we "know" today seems meaningless. It seems to matter so little to the realities of life. O.J. Simpson. Monica-gate. P. Diddy's latest legal problem. Janet's latest wardrobe malfunction. A domestic goddess goes to jail. A fairy-tale princess meets a bloody end. Tom and Katie get married. Britney Spears gets out of rehab. Tom and Katie have a baby. Britney has a baby. Mel Gibson's "Passion of the Christ" is anti-semitic. Mel Gibson's "Passion of the Christ" will save souls. Mel Gibson ties one on and hurls anti-Semitic epithets at cops. The Chair of the House Caucus on Missing and Exploited Children makes passes at Congressional pages. An Evangelical Christian pastor working to pass a Constitutional amendment banning gay marriages turns out himself to be gay. It's not that these stories are uninteresting or unimportant — to someone — although that point is not indefensible, either. But when we are attacked brutally and mercilessly—*for apparently no reason*;

when innocent Americans are killed—*for apparently no reason*; when violence rears its grotesque head—*for apparently no reason*, we are shocked back to reality and ask, "Why do they hate us?" There seems no reasonable explanation other than pure evil and no responsible way to fight it other than war.

But perhaps we've missed something.

Henry Perkinson, in *Getting Better: Television and Moral Progress*, illustrates the many ways in which television acts as a window on the world, revealing to us the good, the bad, and the ugly of the human experience. When we watch televised violence, Perkinson argues, we recoil from it, because that is in our nature. When we see injustice portrayed on television we are outraged and want to see justice prevail. Television portrays the world as it really is, and we can use this external eye to objectively evaluate the state of the world and to improve it.[6]

The civil rights movement of the 1950s and 1960s was helped by the emergence of television. Images of men and women in peaceful protest being beaten by truncheons, attacked by dogs, and swept off their feet by fire hoses, brought home to America the injustices of inequality. The powerful, emotional images entering our homes night after night sparked our sympathy for Americans of African descent and changed our minds about accepting the status quo of Jim Crow segregation.

We "saw the light."

The nightly broadcast of the Vietnam War in the 1960s and 1970s was probably largely responsible for the collapse of American popular support for the war. Images of US Marines lighting the thatched roofs of a village with lighters, of Col. Nguyen Ngoc Loan blowing the brains out of a Viet Cong spy on a Saigon street, of napalm strikes in which South Vietnamese civilians—including children—were mistaken for North Vietnamese troops, and here at home the death of four American college students at Kent State University in Ohio, took a collective toll on the American conscience.

Again, we "saw the light."

But today, far from being a window on the world, Television seems to be becoming—in American culture at least—a mirror. The narcissistic power of material consumption seems to accompany an urge to attend more closely to ourselves than to the outside world. Our mass media outlets are very good at selling things to us—advertising is a $350 billion dollar industry in the US alone[7]—but only, it seems, the things and ideas that we *want* to buy. Our news tends to be sensational and entertaining, and we see little of the outside world. Neil Postman, in his classic critique of television culture *Amusing Ourselves to Death*, calls Americans "the best entertained and quite likely the least well-informed people in the Western world." (p. 106) Viewers, according to Postman, are fed an endless diet of d*isinformation*: "....misplaced, irrelevant, fragmented or superficial information—information that creates the illusion of knowing something but which in fact leads one away from knowing."[8]

Television news, according to Postman, presents us "not only with fragmented news but news without context, without consequences, without value, and therefore without essential seriousness; that is to say, news as pure entertainment."[9] Much of this is the result of the deregulation of the television industry under the Communication Act of 1984 and the emasculation of the FCC under Mark Fowler, a man who believed that television had no greater responsibility to the public than any other home appliance, because TV was just "a toaster with pictures."

Thanks to the Communication Act of 1984 — and subsequent Acts — the present economic structure of television, dependent on advertising revenues for operation, owned by large and wealthy corporations (many of them multinational or even foreign-owned), competing for viewers in an ever-tightening market, unburdened by the requirement to operate in the public interest, ensures that we will consume programming that supports, rather than challenges, the *status quo*. Gone are the days of "Harvest of Shame." The documentary news units of the three major networks before deregulation—ABC, CBS, and NBC—are gone for nearly two decades. One of my first assignments as a young videotape editor for NBC News was working on one of their *last* news documentaries, a profile of Mehmet Ali Agca called "The Man Who Shot the Pope." That was in 1982. Instead, documentary filmmaking has gone independent, and has largely shifted to cable.

Why aren't we angry about that? Why aren't we angry about the diminution of *meaningful* information and *meaningful discourse* in our lives? Why aren't we, like anchorman Howard Beale in Paddy Chayefsky's "Network," opening our windows and crying out to the heavens, "I'm mad as hell, and I'm not going to take it anymore?" Postman asks us, "…what if there are no cries of anguish to be heard? Who is prepared to take arms against a sea of amusements? To whom do we complain, and when, and in what tone of voice, when serious discourse dissolves into giggles? What is the antidote to a culture's being drained by laughter?"[10]

Jacques Ellul, French sociologist, theologian, and media theorist, raises the stakes of the discussion even higher, elevating it to a moral plane. He sees the role of modern media of mass communication as distracting us from the essential evil of our technological society, a society that strips us of our humanity, that separates person from person, that isolates us from our brothers and sisters – and from ourselves. Furthermore, by delivering to us enormous quantities of "facts," mass media encourage us to believe, through a sort of intellectual "sleight of hand," that we know "reality." But we don't; nor do we want to. "In the sphere of the intellectual life," Ellul says, "the major fact of our day is a sort of refusal, unconscious but widespread, to become aware of reality. Man does not want to see himself in the real situation which the world constitutes for him…. The dramatic characteristic of this epoch, in this sphere, is that man no longer grasps anything but shadows. He believes in these shadows, he lives in them, and dies for them. Reality disappears, the reality of man for himself, and the reality of the facts which surround him"[11]

What, then, is the nature of these shadows? And why do they so obscure our "reality?"

Television is a medium of pictures and sounds, of lights and colors and music and movement. It structures information *presentationally* as opposed to the *propositional* structure of speech and writing. That is to say that it recreates or presents to us a mimetic reality, an analog of the human lifeworld. Its content is far more concrete and sensorally understandable than the abstracted experience of, say, a book. Unlike speech or writing, it cannot be stopped or questioned, pored over or studied. It cannot be parsed, criticized grammatically, or put to a test of linear logic. It simply is what it appears to be, nothing more and nothing less. And so critical thought about the televised image is difficult. On an emotional level, we might either like it or hate it. But when we see something, we tend to believe it. In fact, "seeing is believing" is a fair principle to explain our culture.

A logical corollary to this principle, of course, is that *not* seeing is *not* believing. We tend not to believe in those things with which we don't come into contact. Immanence is the milieu of television; transcendence is not. To be sure, Americans give lip service to belief in transcendent ideas, such as God (for instance), but it is not unfair to question the depth of our personal as well as cultural commitment to those ideas. Consider these statistics: 96% of Americans say they believe in God,[12] yet only 45% attend religious services on a weekly basis.[13] Lest we feel too comforted still by that 96%, let's also consider the fact that 36% of Americans believe that astrology is scientific,[14] 50% believe in the reality of UFOs,[15] and 80% believe that the US government is hiding evidence of extraterrestrials.[16]

Television, by focusing our attention so powerfully on our senses, has cut us off from that piece of our psyche that allows us to comprehend the incomprehensible and done tremendous damage to our collective experience of transcendence. Television is so profoundly visual that it has a difficult time dealing with any subject matter that is not itself inherently visual.[17] The sensual, material immanence of our image of reality destroys "transcendence."

"The Light shines in the darkness, and the darkness did not comprehend it."[18]

So what is it, on balance, that we *do* believe in? We believe in those things that are immanent to us in our world. In the world that television creates for us, that appears to be crime and show business.

Our awareness of crime (our "belief" in it, if you will) seems to exist disproportionately to its commission. Throughout the 1990s, violent crime rates dropped 6% from a decade earlier, and homicides dropped 13%. Yet, in a series of ABC News/ Washington Post polls during the same period, six times more Americans (30%) named crime as America's biggest problem in 1993 than did in 1992.[19] In fact, during the 1990's the reporting of crime eclipsed the reporting of all other stories, totaling some 7448 stories between 1993 and 1996, more reports than were aired on the war in Bosnia, the 1996 Presidential campaign, the plight of post-Soviet Russia, and the Israeli-Palestinian conflict *combined*.[20]

The number of stories dedicated to show business has risen dramatically too since the early 1990s. More entertainment stories (868) were aired between 1992 and 1997 than were aired on such important topics as the environment (561) and education (464).[21]

And while stories on crime, disasters, and war dominate our information environment, accounting for some 40% of all news coverage[22], precious little reporting on international political and economic stories is done. Such reporting might help us to understand the relationships between peoples and nations that cause wars, and could motivate us to take political action to intervene diplomatically or economically before wars break out. But in the Tower of Babble that we call the "information age," a critical and objective view of the world and our place within it is replaced by a chaotic, discordant onslaught of meaningless "facts."

Even though wars are big on television, not all wars infiltrate our consciousness. Where the United States or its allies or interests are not involved, war does not seem to exist for us. The Department of Peace and Conflict Research at Uppsala University in Sweden report that on average 9 minor armed conflicts (where the number of deaths does not exceed 1000 during the course of the conflict), 12 intermediate armed conflicts (where the number of deaths exceeds 1000, but is fewer than 1000 in any given year), and 13 wars (with more than 1000 deaths a year) go on at all times somewhere in the world.

In the year 2000, war took the lives of 168,000 Africans, 65,000 Asians, 39,000 "middle-easterners," 37,000 Europeans, and 2,000 Central and South Americans.[23] At the same time, American arms manufacturers were making it possible for war to be the "booming business" that it is. Forty of the top one hundred arms-producing companies in the world are American companies with profits totaling $664 billion dollars in 1999. Nearly $217 billion of that amount ($216,730,000,000.00) comes from the American manufacture and sale of weapons ($93 billion in 1999), more than the profit of the other 60 companies combined.[24] Is this not something Americans should know about?

Meanwhile, those in the less technologically developed world who are not dying in warfare are likely to be dying of disease or starvation. While the life expectancy of the average American was about 78 years in 2008, it was 70 for the Indonesian, 65 for the Russian, 44 for the Afghan (down from 45 years in 2001 – has "liberation" helped?), 39 for the Zambian, and 38 for the Rwandan and the Mozambiquan.[25] While an American baby has 99.4% chance of survival after birth, the infant mortality rate is 2% for the Russian, 10% for the Ethiopian, almost 15% for the Afghan, and nearly 20% for the Angolan.[26]

And while much of the "third world" believes that we care little for their welfare, many more question our motivations even less kindly. They believe we are more interested in exploiting their natural resources for our benefit, and exploiting them for their cheap labor.

Among the violations of the fair labor conventions of the International Labor Organization between 1996 and 2000, were many committed on behalf of American companies.

Some examples:

- Factories in the Northern Mariana Islands (a US Commonwealth) that produce clothing for Abercrombie & Fitch, Cutter & Buck, Donna Karan, The GAP, J. Crew, Levi Strauss, Liz Claiborne, Nordstrom, Ralph Lauren Polo, Target, Dress Barn, and Tommy Hilfiger demand contracts of their workers which: waive basic human rights including the right to join a union; demand 12-hour workdays seven days-a-week; subject workers to "lockdowns" in the factory;

- Factories in China producing clothing and shoes for Adidas, Disney, Fila, Nike, Ralph Lauren, and Reebok employ forced labor in prison camps; demand of their employees 12-16 hour workdays, seven days-a-week; employ child labor; demand forced overtime; and Chinese workers for Nestle have been subjected to electric shock to maintain productivity.

- Factories in Indonesia manufacturing clothing and shoes for Adidas, the GAP, and Nike subject workers to forced overtime at a poverty wage.

- Factories in El Salvador producing clothing and shoes for Adidas, Ann Taylor, the GAP, Liz Claiborne and Nike pay their female employees about US$30/week for a 60-80 hour week; subject their female workers to forced pregnancy tests; fire their female workers if they become pregnant; and force some employees to work overtime without pay, up to 11 hours a day.

- Factories in Haiti producing clothing and toys for the Walt Disney Company pay their workers an average of US$2.40 per day, and charge them for transportation ($.66/day), breakfast (cornmeal and fruit juice – $.53/ day), and lunch (rice and beans – $.66/day).

- Factories in Russia producing clothing for the GAP pay their employees US$.11/hour.[27]

If terrorism is evil—and it is—this is terror's recruiting station.

But, apparently, *none of these things qualifies as news!* We are kept in the dark about such ugly, painful realities, but delivered "facts" on a daily basis about Britney, K-Fed, Tom and Katie, and Madonna. *"What we don't know can't hurt us..."* But if we are, on the whole, ignorant of the realities of the world, we know on another level that there is suffering out there. We know there is poverty. We know there is exploitation. We know. And we ignore it.

In the 1980s Lester C. Thurow argued that true economic and social equality demanded a fundamental restructuring of the economy. The "zero-sum" concept reflects a growing global ecological understanding that we cannot have great wealth as a nation without taking it from someone else. The "game" of Capitalism, as currently played, is a zero-sum game. Corporations amass wealth at the expense of other corporations. National economies flourish at the expense of other national economies. Competition rather than cooperation is at the center of the zero-sum conception of capitalist economics. But it does not have to be at the center of capitalism.

To at least a certain extent, Adam Smith was fooling himself, and we know it. We've known it (at least) since the time of Karl Marx. Communism is dead, and rightly so, for it denied the essential freedom and dignity of the human person. But an economic system without strict regulation also denies the essential imperfection of the human person. Greed exists. Envy exists. Hatred exists. Not just in the hearts and minds of our "enemies," but in ours as well. They are part of our reality.

I think I probably need, at this point, to assert as strongly as possible that I believe in three great American "myths": the myth of American goodness (as inherent in our Americanism), the myth of American generosity, and the myth of Capitalism (as solution to social justice problems). These myths work themselves through our conscious, rational minds in a manner something like the following: "We're good people and a good nation. We give so much to other nations. Our wealth and our goodness allow us to be generous. We are *unusually* generous people. Everyone wants to be like us. Everyone wants to come to America."

These American myths are true until we come to believe in them to such an extent that we can no longer see that there are exceptions to them all around us. In a sense, we wash our hands of the reality of life outside the United States by focusing on things—truths?—in the abstract. We dismiss any sense of a *present* global responsibility by reminding ourselves of what we have done, and have been in the *past*.

We tend to neglect—no, to ignore with impunity—much of the poverty, disease, deprivation, and death of the third world while at the same time we expect them to provide the raw materials and fuel that run our economy and give us the wealth we enjoy on a daily basis. And then we have the audacity as a nation to ask, "Why do they hate us?" Could it not be because, by all outward appearances, we hate *them?* Well, we don't hate them. Nor, for that matter, do we love them, or even care about them. We hardly know "they" exist. And that, I suggest, is the real problem.

Our postmodern universe of entertaining images and sounds, of uncertainty about any but personal, subjective experience, of an abandonment of belief in objective truth, and of doubt and confusion about transcendence has created, and serves as, a thought model for 21st century America. We are dazed and confused, entertained and amused, and don't know what to do about it – or whether we should even try.

In order to try to address these difficulties, I would at this point like to go out on a limb and stray a bit from the media ecological and into an area where I claim no real authority but have some ideas — a theology of communication. I would like to offer to you what I call a "Trinitarian" model of communication.

The Trinitarian conception of Deity sees "three persons" in one God: the "Father," the Son and the Holy Spirit. God the Father – creator of "all that is seen and unseen," who "so loved the world that he gave His only begotten Son; " God the Son — the Logos, the Word Incarnate, fully human and fully Divine; and God the Holy Spirit—the loving relationship between Creator and all creation.

A Trinitarian conception of communication would need to recreate or resemble this model. Unlike the traditional and well-known model of communication which includes a sender, a receiver, a message, and a medium, a "Trinitarian" conception of communication would situate in dynamic relationship a Creator (the sender of the message), the message itself (a "creation" of the sender, and necessarily being of the same essence—i.e., a "truthful" expression of the sender), and, most importantly, a particular type of context, i.e., a sincere and genuine love and concern on the part of the creator/sender for the integrity of her message and for the welfare of her "audience."

At the risk of sounding arrogant, I'd like to suggest that "real" human communication occurs *only* when such sincere and genuine love and concern exist between participants in the communication act. Anything else may be communication in a lesser form—the maintenance of control or orientation, for example, or the initiation of a stimulus/response chain that helps us fulfill our needs—but should not be thought of as real human communication. Only ***compassionate love*** yields real human communication.

I see this Trinitarian conception of communication reflected in many social institutions—in marriage and in the family, for instance. In friendship. I see it in the social institutions of religion and education. You probably see, as I do, powerful evidence of it in here at Dominican University.

But I also see it, from time to time, absent from all these institutions and see some other motivation than mutual care and concern, some other motivation than ***caritas*** taking over. At such times, I believe, we are in jeopardy; our very humanity, perhaps, is in jeopardy.

Lack of interest in communication yields inaccuracy and incompleteness and results in chaos. Self-interest in communication yields deliberate distraction from the truth and results in manipulation. Egoistic self-interest yields lies and falsehood and results in totalitarian control. Emphasis on communication within and throughout an institution rather than among the individuals who constitute it yields rigid formalism and results in cynicism, demoralization, and hopelessness. Only a shared context of mutual respect, care, and concern for the other results in true human communication. And I further suggest to you that when our societal systems of mass communication assume profit rather than the common good as their motivation, there is no love, and there is no real human communication.

Marshall McLuhan, the (nearly) legendary media philosopher and prophet of the age of electronic communication—now enjoying something of a Renaissance in the academic circles of communication study—is probably best remembered for his intriguing and somewhat mysterious aphorism, "the medium is the message." McLuhan scholars still argue over the meaning of this phrase.

Whatever McLuhan's specific intentions, I like to think that this aphorism can be applied to the communitarian conception of communication. The medium (truth) *is* the message (communication taking place within a context of compassionate love). Furthermore, the meaning of compassion is made clear in the idea of true communication – a sharing of the experiences of life with another. Where there is true communication, because there is true compassion, medium and message come together and are one, creating a cosmic *ecology of love*, if only we have the eyes to see, the ears to hear, and the good will to believe.

At the same time that McLuhan was teaching and writing at St. Michael's College at the University of Toronto, a great American was teaching the world about communication from within a communitarian framework. He was trying to get Americans to step out of the darkness of racial bigotry and comfortable complacency and into the light of love. The Rev. Dr. Martin Luther King, Jr., in a sermon delivered at the

National Cathedral in Washington, D.C. in 1968 told us:

> Through our scientific and technological genius, we have
> made of this world a neighborhood and yet we have not
> had the ethical commitment to make of it a brotherhood.
> But somehow, and in some way, we have got to do this.
> We must all learn to live together as brothers or we will
> all perish together as fools....We are tied together in
> the single garment of destiny, caught in an inescapable
> network of mutuality. And whatever affects one directly
> affects all indirectly. For some strange reason I can never
> be what I ought to be until you are what you ought to
> be. And you can never be what you ought to be until I
> am what I ought to be. This is the way God's universe
> is made; this is the way it is structured...John Donne
> caught it years ago and placed it in graphic terms: "No
> man is an island entire of itself. Every man is a piece
> of the continent, a part of the main...Any man's death
> diminishes me because I am involved in mankind;
> therefore never send to know for whom the bell tolls;
> it tolls for thee."...We must see this, believe this, and
> live by it if we are to remain awake through a great
> revolution....We are challenged to rid our nation and the
> world of poverty.[28]

In order to take up that challenge, we must—in the first
place—be aware of the world, be engaged in it, be more open
to the reality of the event than we are to its "instant replay."
Turn off the computer, turn off the Playstation, turn off the
CD player, the DVD player, the VCR; turn off the television.
Turn off that eerie blue glow that each evening threatens
to envelop our homes in darkness. Turn off the allure of
material consumption, the temptations of physical comfort,
the distractions of the technological society, and turn on the
light in our hearts. At the same time, we must demand the truth
from those in positions of authority in our social institutions.
We must never sit by complacently or deferentially when

legitimate authority yields to information control.

We can change the ways we relate to the world, and we can change the world. We can lift up poorer people and nations, and make a safer world. For where there is real human communication—where there is love—there can be no terror.

The truth is out there…we must choose – there is no other alternative – to either see it, live it, and if necessary, fix it…. or we must choose to remain, as we are now, in the dark.

ENDNOTES

1. The Catholic University of America, *The New Catholic Encyclopedia,* second edition (Washington, D.C.: The Catholic University of America and Thomson/Gale Publishing Co., 2003), vol. 7, p. 314.

2. Ibid., p. 315.

3. Ibid.

4. Ibid.

5. 1 John 2:11, paraphrased

6. Henry Perkinson, *Getting Better: Television and Moral Progress* (New Brunswick: Transaction Publishers, 1991).

7. Dictionary of Critical Sociology On-Line: http://www. public. iastate.edu/~rmazur/dictionary/a.html

8. Neil Postman, *Amusing Ourselves to Death: Public Discourse in the Age of Show Business* (New York: Penguin Books, 1985), p. 106.

9. Ibid., p. 100.

10. Ibid., p. 156.

11. Jacques Ellul, *The Presence of the Kingdom* (Colorado Springs: Helmers and Howard, 1989), pp.81-82.

12. US News On-Line (*http://www.usnews.com/usnews/issue/001023/23atlarge.htm*).

13. University of Michigan News and Information Service (http://www.umich.edu/~newsinfo/releases/1997/dec97/r121097a. html)

14. National Science Foundation survey cited in "Galileo would be spinning in his grave," by Tony Blankley, Reporter-News.com (http://www.reporternews.com/2000/opinion/blank0715.html)

15. Parascope: On-Line Journal of the Paranormal (http://www. parascope.com/articles/0597/gallup.htm)

16. "Alien crashes into desert! Starts life of its own!" by M. Mitchell Waldrop, Ph.D., on Discovery.com (http://www.discovery. com/area/roswell/roswellNEW.html)

17. Postman, op. cit., p. 27.

18. John 1:5-14

19. John Sheehan, Press Release from the Center for Media and Public Affairs, March 4, 1994, cited in *Media Monitor*

20. "IN 1990s TV NEWS TURNS TO VIOLENCE AND SHOW BIZ," (Press Release), The Center for Media and Public Affairs, August 12, 1997. (http://www.cmpa.com/pressrel/mm78pr.htm)

21. Ibid.

22. Paul Klite, Robert A. Bardwell, and Jason Salzman, "Pavlov's TV Dog: A Snapshot of Local TV News in America Taken on September 20, 1995. Rocky Mountain Media Watch Content Analysis #7. Rocky Mountain Media Watch, Denver Colorado.

23. *The World Health Report 2001* (Geneva: The World Health Organization, 2001), pp. 148-149. While no Americans were killed in active warfare in 2000, we should not necessarily assume that we were at peace. In the year 2000, 66,000 Americans took their own lives.

24. "The 100 largest arms-producing companies in the OECD and developing countries," data sheet, Stockholm International Peace Research Institute (This summary doesn't include joint American/ foreign corporations such as DaimlerChrysler and DaimlerChrysler Aerospace who alone made US$6 billion in arms sales in 1999). (http://projects.sipri.se/milex/aprod/sipridata.html)

25. *The World Health Report 2001*, pp. 137-159.

26. "Comparative International Statistics," Statistical Abstract of the United States, (Washington: United States Census Bureau, 2001), p. 835.

27. "Violations of the ILO conventions (International Labor Organization)" (http://www.transnationale.org/anglais/transnationale /tiersmonde/bit.htm)

28. King, Martin Luther, Jr., "Remaining Awake through a Great Revolution," sermon delivered at the National Cathedral, Washington, DC, 31 March 1968 (in Congressional Record, 9 April 1968).

Peter K. Fallon: An Interview[ii]

Laureano Ralon: How did you decide to become a university professor? Was it a conscious choice?

Peter K. Fallon: Of course it was, at some point. The problem was not so much one of decision as of discernment, of seeing the various choices that were, in fact, before me. We do not live in a culture that much values either education or educators, and many young people will choose a pay check (especially a nice fat one) over a life that offers rewards more spiritual and intellectual than pecuniary. Thirty-five or forty years ago I had no idea I'd be doing what I'm doing today. And I probably would have laughed at the prospect. But the cumulative effect of my life experiences over the years pointed me in a direction and provided me with evidence that it was the right direction. I once thought I'd be a musician (my first college major was music theory) and later I wanted to be a recording engineer. My first real job was making educational and training videotapes

[ii]Figure/Ground is a web-based project created by Laureano Ralon, the founder and driving force of Figure/Ground Communication. He is a graduate of Simon Fraser University School of Communication, where he earned his bachelor's and master's degrees under the supervision of Brian Lewis and Roman Onufrijchuk. Laureano has worked as a teaching assistant for SFU's Center for Online and Distance Education, and as a research assistant for the Center for Policy Research on Science and Technology, the New Media Innovation Center, and the 2006 Telecommunications Policy Review Panel. He graciously granted permission to publish this interview. This series includes interviews with Eric McLuhan, Elizabeth Eisenstein, Noam Chomsky, Douglas Rushkoff, and many others. You can find this interview and others at: http://figureground.ca/interviews/peter-k-fallon/ Dr. Fallon was interviewed by Laureano Ralon on December 30th, 2010. © Peter K. Fallon and Figure/Ground Communications

for the New York State Office of Mental Health, and then I spent nearly two decades with NBC News. But all during this time I was in and out of school (mostly in, in retrospect), working first on a Master's degree in Communication, and then on my Doctorate in Media Ecology. And I loved every moment I spent in the classroom as a student.

I had some opportunities to teach as an adjunct along the way and I loved sharing what I was learning, especially in my work at NYU, with my own students. My own teaching, I hope, is influenced by some of my best teachers who were able not only to give me objective information but were also able to convey (or, perhaps, unable *not* to convey) their fascination with a subject. And unlike my work with NBC, which was seen on a daily basis by several million people to whom I remained completely anonymous, and whose effects on those millions of people I shudder to think about, my work with a handful of students was immediately gratifying, immensely rewarding, and unambiguously positive: I help them to *see* things deeply embedded in their culture that were previously invisible to them, and I help them to *think* about those things through systems of critical thought they had never encountered before this class.

One last point about this particular conscious choice: in order to accept the offer of my first full-time teaching position, I had to leave NBC News and take an enormous cut in pay. To be precise, I took a $60,000.00 cut in pay. I can assure you I didn't make this decision lightly or without deep, deep reflection. And it is not something I am bragging about; most people thought I was nuts. So I had a whole series of conscious choices to make along the way. Eventually and inevitably, I believe, they were all leading me to teach. It would have been a terrible personal tragedy for me to have ignored all the experiences I had in the course of this journey.

LR: Joshua Meyrowitz' thesis in No Sense of Place is that when media change, situations and roles change. In your experience, how did the role of university professor evolve since you were an undergraduate student?

PKF: Well, that's the funny thing about "the social construction of reality," isn't it? Reality never changes. It is our attitudes about reality that change. Technologies play an enormous role in our socially-constructed reality because they are the media that constitute the message of our society. New media restructure human relationships and therefore human priorities. They restructure both the things we think about (or not) and how we think about them. Media, as Neil Postman said, are epistemologies. But they are epistemologies with firm ontological foundations – they are extensions of our senses (or, in the case of most of our media, only two of our five senses). We tend to know what is real to us and what does not appear to be real we ignore. And so roles change because situations *appear* to have changed because our media have changed.

But what has changed? The truth is that nothing changes. As it says in Ecclesiastes (1:9), "What has been will be again, what has been done will be done again; there is nothing new under the sun." Or as Shakespeare put it (Sonnet 59), "If there be nothing new, but that which is hath been before, how are our brains beguiled…" It is *we* who have changed, *we* who are beguiled by technological change, *we* who have ceased to believe that a certain situation exists while beginning to believe a new one has replaced it. We still love and hate, suffer and feel joy, resent and admire, covet and sacrifice. We still allow some with power to exploit and marginalize others without power, and we still look on quietly, feeling bad about it all but doing nothing. Nothing at all changes when new technologies are introduced into a culture. Nothing changes but our attitudes about what is and is not "real," what is and is not "important," what is and is not worth knowing. And we change because we choose to change, because media, as McLuhan tells us, are nothing more than extensions of *us*.

It could not be any other way. One of the things I have grappled with over the years (as do most media ecologists) is the problem of technological determinism. The term is frequently tossed around quite carelessly, I think, and many times is so tossed in lieu of a reasoned argument against theories of technology and social change. But still it is there – the accusation: *determinist!* – and the serious media scholar will consider the possibility that a certain idea is, after all, deterministic. I have always been a believer in two truths, one immanent and one transcendent: the virtually limitless potential of human intelligence and the possibility of free will. Anyone who believes in either of those truths – but especially anyone who believes in them both – will seek other explanations for phenomena than deterministic ones. Nothing *has to* be. Whatever *is* is because we've either actively made it so, or allowed it to exist without our resistance.

All of this is to say that many of the role changes we've seen and experienced in academia – and in "the real world" – are entirely unnecessary, a reaction to nothing more than an appearance of change, and a more or less unquestioned assumption of the reality of that change, that has become part of a socially-constructed (as opposed to objective) reality. What I thought was important as an undergraduate student three and a half decades ago is still important today. The basics never change. It's really as simple as that.

When I was an undergrad, those "best teachers" I referred to in the previous question were concerned with making me think, and making me think critically, and they provided a framework of theoretical knowledge and principles derived from that knowledge to help me do so.

They demanded that I read. It didn't matter whether I thought the text they were making me read was "relevant" to my life or not. They knew that I was in no real position to make such a determination. They knew that the relevance of a text would not necessarily be apparent to a young person of eighteen, nineteen, or twenty years. Relevance can be judged only in the light of experience, never decided beforehand. Such a decision reflects culturally manufactured desires, not a mature acknowledgement of human needs.

They demanded that I not only have an opinion (for who

on this earth has no opinion?) but that I be able to support that opinion with reasoned argument, logic, and evidence, and role modeled behavior that gave me the confidence to be tolerant of other opinions, but unafraid to question and challenge them.

They demanded meticulous care in my use of words. Words, I learned, were the brick and mortar of reason. Every rational judgment I made would be made in words and expressed in words and I'd better strive for precision or be prepared to live with sloppy thought and poor communication skills.

But equally significant in my experience, my best teachers also showed me that they cared about human communication, that it is fundamental to our humanity, and that it is important enough to study it so that we can not only understand human interaction (for all human behavior is symbolic) but also improve it when it falls short.

That was what my best professors did four decades ago, and that is what I believe the best professors do today. None of this has changed. This is objective reality. But all of this kind of begs your question which is essentially that in our socially-constructed reality, new media have presented to us new roles and redefined relationships requiring new "skill sets" and ways of learning. And I believe – and there is an awful lot of objective data that supports this belief – that it is our acceptance of these presumed new roles and relationships that accounts for at least some of the failures in American education in the last few decades.

As I write this, I have learned that one of the greatest teachers I've ever known, my mentor and dissertation chair at NYU Christine Nystrom, died yesterday (December 22, 2010). I am saddened by this news almost beyond words. It is difficult to explain just what Chris meant to me as a young scholar full of questions and uncertainty. She embodied the qualities I'm talking about and inspires me still to provide my students with the lessons she gave me: observe, question, think critically, think clearly, write clearly, and above all *care*. If we ever allow the role of university professor to "evolve" beyond these simple ideas, then God help us.

LR: What makes a good teacher today? What advice would you give to young graduate students and aspiring university professors?

PKF: I believe I've already answered that, although I certainly admit that most people today would be inclined to argue against my point. What makes a good teacher today is what has always made a good teacher: command of a subject, a critical mind, a demanding nature, and an ability to inspire students to pursue knowledge for some end beyond mere financial rewards. A good teacher might be entertaining and funny, but shouldn't set out to be. A good teacher may have broad experience with and skills using technology, but the mere possession of such experience and skills doesn't make one a good teacher.

My advice to people who want to teach is pretty simple and very likely to be ridiculed: *don't believe the bullshit.* You're not there to help students get skills for a workplace. You're not there to make them more marketable. You're not there to provide them with answers to petty, superficial questions. You're not there to impress them – or yourself – with the latest technological wonder that promises to make something "better" but will probably only shorten some algorithmic process and benefit an employer. You're not there to mass produce replaceable parts for the machinery of the global economy. You're there for one reason and one reason only: to make them better people than they were when they came in.

In order to do this, you'll have to push them, prod them, cajole them, anger them, question them, and make them question themselves and their own previously unquestioned assumptions about the world. You'll have to butt heads with your colleagues, your school, your administrators. You'll have to be prepared to explain yourself to others who will want to know why you appear so out of synch with your culture. It's not easy, so you'd better get used to it.

Or, like far too many university professors today, you can aspire to nothing more than merely cranking out more cogged wheels for the machine, being a servant of the technological society.

As usual, the choice is ours to make.

LR: Let's change the topic. I know you are a practicing Catholic, as was Marshall McLuhan. I also know that, prior to heading to New York Institute of Technology and later NYU, you attended Maria Regina Diocesan High School. How did your Christian beliefs influence your career trajectory, your research interests, and your view of communication studies as a discipline?

PKF: I'll go you one further: I went to Catholic grammar school too, Cure of Arts School in Merrick, New York. I was educated by Dominican sisters in both grammar school and high school, and eventually spent ten years teaching alongside them at Molloy College in Rockville Centre, New York. My wife Mary Pat and I are both Dominican Associates – lay members of the "Ordinis Praedicatorum" – the Order of Preachers.

But I think it is dangerous to look at someone's religion or their religious background or their upbringing in general and assume, "Ah-HAH! That's why they came out the way they did," as though two children of the same parents raised in the same household can be expected to think and act the same. On the contrary, it took me years – decades – to "find my faith" and I'm still working on a day-to-day basis to figure out what that faith means. Indeed, your question misquotes me. I usually describe myself as "a practicing Catholic, and I'm going to keep practicing until I get it right."

I'm actually a very bad Catholic, or so I have been told by people who define themselves as "good Catholics." I come into conflict with my Church in a number of areas (it is not necessary to detail them here). While I don't agree at all with the category or the label attached to it, I am considered by some a "cafeteria Catholic," which is to say I have real problems with (among other things) the principle of Papal infallibility and patriarchal structure and tend to choose which teachings sound to me to be authentic reflections of Divine will and which ones seem little more than the whims of fallible humans (men, to be clear). I'm not proud of this tendency and I constantly question my own motivations for thinking as I do, but I am in no way ashamed of it either. It is part of the person I am and if there is a God (and I believe strongly that God exists) then I would be doing an injustice to that God's creative power to be anything or anyone other than what and who I am. For better or for worse – and may God forgive me for my arrogance – I will not be swayed by the teachings, the traditions, or "the magisterium" of a faith simply because the culture that faith engendered and continues to support says I must be. I need more than that.

So, no, I don't think my faith influenced my career trajectory, my research interests, or my attraction to the ideas constituting the meta-discipline of Media Ecology. I think some part of me that I can't describe, that I can't really be certain even exists, that doesn't reside in any organ or system of my body, but that still makes me who I am influenced my interests, made me see Media Ecology as a system of investigation uniquely suited to examining interactions of technology and culture *and* eventually led me to a place where I felt compelled to embrace a particular faith. Again, I don't see anything – not a technology, not a culture, not a language, not a religion – as having that sort of power. That, to me, smacks of determinism. I'm not quite as convinced that we are not *genetically* predisposed toward or against certain attitudes, stances, strengths and weaknesses, etc., but that's another story. What I'm saying is that I *chose* Media Ecology, I *chose* what subjects interest me, and I *chose* my faith – and all of these choices came after decades of questioning, longing for answers, uncertainty, confusion, etc. And I continue to choose them on a daily basis.

LR: In 1999, Eric McLuhan edited an interesting book with a provocative title – The Medium and the Light: Reflections on Religion. Is God the Light?

PKF: Well, that question just packs metaphor upon metaphor,

doesn't it? Both the word and the idea of "God" are metaphors for something we can't begin either to understand or to even imagine. "God" is the purest act of the human imagination, arguably the earliest of our inventions. Pure metaphor. And "light" or, even better, "*the* light" is a metaphor perhaps even more primal than God. So you're asking me, in essence, if one metaphor constitutes another metaphor. My answer is yes, metaphorically speaking.

What is the use of "God" if not to stand as a metaphor for the goodness that human beings find in the core of their own beings? "God" is goodness and right. "God" is creation and, by extension, the creative urge. "God" is the organizing principle of the universe, the "logos," the Divine, Cosmic wisdom, negative entropy: perfect and unbounded love. "The light" is the good, the opposite of darkness (and, therefore, by extension, of ignorance), the source of life, provider of warmth and security. Light is truth. And the source of light (metaphorically speaking) is love.

So of course there are multiple layers of overlapping meanings between these two metaphors and it should come as no surprise that we'll use one metaphor to explain another. I have no problem saying, within this context, that "God is the light" any more than I would saying "God is love."

I myself exploit this metaphor in the last chapter of *The Metaphysics of Media*, "In the Dark: The Survival of Ignorance in an Age of Information." Darkness symbolizes ignorance and fear, fear and ignorance support hatred, a heart filled with fear and hatred is a "heart of darkness," and so on. By contrast, light has always been a metaphor for learning. Light is certainly closely physically connected with reading. In cartoons, the light bulb switching on over a character's head symbolizes a "eureka moment" – all of a sudden, the character has had an important realization. And I have no qualms about using these two complementary metaphors and, further, letting the reader assume – correctly – that I'm making a moral judgment about ignorance – particularly voluntary ignorance, or what Catholic theology calls "vincible ignorance": ignorance about a thing or phenomenon that we could easily dispel if we cared enough.

LR: Indeed, the electric light has always been a privileged medium to media ecologists. For instance, at one point in the documentary Picnic in Space, McLuhan turns on a flashlight and remarks that light does not have a point of view; that it radiates in all directions at once, having a spherical, auditory character. In fact, he believed that the electric light was the only medium that had no content – the only medium whereby medium and message were the same. This is very phenomenological, I think. Unlike the empiricist notion of consciousness as a passive absorption of sensory impressions bombarding us from the external world, the phenomenologists regarded consciousness as transcendental, i.e., as pointing outward into the world. In a sense, both the electric light and consciousness could be viewed as a sort of nothingness, following Sartre. Consciousness, by way of intentionality, emerges attracted by something other than itself, while the electric light becomes transparent and withdraws from our conscious awareness to create an environment that allows us to focus upon things other than itself. Aren't our invisible environments then, much like consciousness, a kind of room-making nothingness which pierces through the heart of being?

PKF: Neil Postman talked at great length about technology answering the question "*How* do we do something?" but that it was up to philosophy – particularly the field of ethics – to answer the question "*Why* do we do something?" The history of science, in general, is the history of our growing understanding of the physical world, and empiricism has played a central role in this process. The history of technology is the history of applying that understanding of the material world to solve some sort of problem. The history of philosophy is the history of human groping for meaning in the raw data of material reality. But raw data presents itself to us as more or less objective, and meaning can appear very, very personal.

All of this is to say that I'm not sure I can answer your question satisfactorily in the way you asked it. It is, to be frank, something of a loaded question, and in order to answer it I have accept some premises that I'm not prepared to accept. McLuhan's observations about electric light (like all of McLuhan's observations) are not terribly objective and don't lend themselves to empirical investigation. That is both their weakness and their strength, as Lance Strate has reminded me time and time again by emphasizing the heuristic playfulness of "the probe." The fact that electric light is *pure* content (rather than having *no* content) is an illustration of McLuhan's aphorism "the medium is the message" – the significance of electric light is its restructuring of the day and of the traditional human understanding of time and its utility. With this I certainly agree.

But no artificial light is omni-directional; it is in the nature of artificial light to exist in artificial space, and there is always something or someone holding on to it or hanging it. There is no three-hundred-sixty degrees (cubed) with artificial light. We might also consider the laser which is focused electric light, a single point rather than an infinite number of points (cubed) and is nothing if not subjective. Point of view is part and parcel of artificial light, and let's not fool ourselves into thinking otherwise regardless of McLuhan's heuristic and playful (if sometimes dangerous and misleading) eloquence.

Nor does light resemble consciousness, I believe, in the way you suggest. Despite the most devout wishes of phenomenologists, human beings don't "radiate" consciousness. I honestly wish we did. If human consciousness were like radar – another form of light – and radiated out from us and brought back to us impressions of things of which we would not otherwise be aware, we would be, as a species, a lot better off than we are now. Consciousness is indeed intentional and that is both the strength and the weakness of human intelligence. For our intention can be to use our technologies to build a comprehensive understanding of our world and to address its problems, or our intention can be to use our technologies to create our own comfortable, self-sufficient, solipsistic worlds and to ignore the objective reality that surrounds us. I write at some length about this in my book *The Metaphysics of Media*.

The point of all of this is merely to note that McLuhan was engaging in metaphor, I believe, to illustrate something that was difficult to express in objective, literal terms. And so was Plato, and Aristotle, and Aquinas, and Descartes, and Kant, and Hegel, and Husserl, and Sartre. Or if they weren't intentionally engaging in metaphor then we must understand that they ought to have realized that their ideas were, in fact, models – metaphors – that attempted to explain the interplay of matter, imagination, and mind but were doomed to be pale, inadequate reflections of a reality that we are not, at this moment, fully able to comprehend. Each of these metaphors focuses our attention on a specific dimension of human experience. They are neither entirely wrong nor entirely right.

LR: What can you tell us about your most recent book, The Metaphysics of Media? Other than the invisible effects and environments that media ecologists strive to raise to awareness, what 'exactly' is metaphysical about media?

PKF: Nothing. Not a thing.

Again, media are really nothing more than extensions of us. It is *we*, not the media, who are metaphysical. Metaphysics is part and parcel of an organ – the human brain – that processes information both propositionally and presentationally, in words and in images; in reason and in imagination. We believe and refuse to believe. We believe in things that have no physical nature, no material reality, and we refuse to believe in them. We believe in things that not only have a physical, material nature but are also empirically measurable, and we refuse to believe in them. And our media play a role in all of this.

The Metaphysics of Media is predicated on the observation that different media throughout human history have engendered and supported different conceptions of reality and, consequently, un-reality. That's the ontology. They have also been central to evolving human understandings of *how* we know things, and what things are worth knowing. That's the epistemology involved in the question of a medium's metaphysical orientation.

It is difficult, in a few short paragraphs, to go into the argument in great depth or to cite the evidence I provide in some detail in the book. But I'll give a thumbnail sketch: the era of primary orality is marked by animism and monistic pantheism; a single realm of reality imbued with the supernatural. Magic, science and religion (to cite Malinowski's title) intermingle as immanent reality and transcendent reality appear inseparable.

The development of writing systems – especially the alphabetic – and the onset of literacy create a rift between immanent and transcendent experiences. Oral tales of transcendent experience become sacred scripture and orthodoxies are formed, while at the very same time the fixity of speech in space lends objective distance to thought (as Walter Ong pointed out). The rift deepens and expands as literacy itself deepens and expands following the development of movable-type printing. Three "camps" appear, each one championing its preferred metaphysical orientation: those who believe only in an immanent reality (natural philosophers, scientists, etc.), those who believe in a dualistic reality with the transcendent trumping the immanent (theologians), and those who desperately try to bridge the gap between faith and reason (Thomists).

In the technologically-developed west, the breach between transcendence and immanence becomes irrelevant in the era of electricity as transcendence itself all but disappears. Propositional structures of thought fall to the presentational, reason gives way to emotion, fixed, objective point of view cedes to subjective personal experience, internal experience yields to external, sensory experience, a "secondary orality" arises. We fine-tune our technologies to bring us only the information we want, and ignore much of the objective reality of those parts of the world (the vast majority, in fact) who do not enjoy the same level of development as we do.

At every point, I must emphasize, our technologies act as instruments of our will. There is no determinism involved. If Americans are largely ignorant of the world, it is not the fault of the media that saturate our lives. It is because we choose our ignorance, and use those media to facilitate it.

LR: You are an active member of the Media Ecology Association. How did media ecology as a subfield within the larger discipline of communication studies evolve since you were a doctoral student at NYU?

PKF: I am at the moment an active member of the MEA and certainly wish to remain so. I was not always so active and can't really predict what the future holds in store for me. The "vicissitudes of life" and all that… Others have been far more active than I have and are largely responsible for shaping this organization into what I believe is an incredibly important "clearinghouse" for scholarship and collaboration. Lance Strate, Thom Gencarelli, Janet Sternberg, Jim Morrison and so many others have been there since the beginning and we all owe them a great debt. They can describe in far greater detail the evolution of the MEA as well as the meta-discipline of media ecology.

For my part, I'm not sure that media ecology, as a meta-discipline, has evolved at all. There has always been a fluidity, a flexibility, in both perspectives and methodologies, that allows for a very high degree of creative and critical thought. McLuhan's probes are both philosophy and literature – with, perhaps, a bit of theology hidden within, Ellul blends sociology and theology, Innis looks at communication as an economic activity and technologies as media of exchange, Mary Ann Wolf (although I'm not sure anyone has yet told her she is a media ecologist) gave us our first neurological study of literacy that is, at the same time, a deeply philosophical work. Stanislas Dehaene's wonderful book *Reading in the Brain* extends and deepens Mary Ann Wolf's neurological connections. Elizabeth

Eisenstein's historical approach influenced the work I did on my first book, *Why the Irish Speak English*, and even *The Metaphysics of Media*, while it attempts (and I emphasize the word *attempts*) the sort of cultural criticism so masterfully achieved by Jacques Ellul and Neil Postman, is very historical in its approach.

So I see no real evolution in media ecology beyond the "shape shifting" nature that seems to have been deliberately embedded in its fabric. The one thing that must, I think, always define a study we recognize as media ecological is its acknowledgement of the interactions of cultures – and the people who constitute those cultures – and their technologies.

LR: Do you think that media ecology will ever attain the status of a discipline, concerned as it is with invisible media effects and environments – again, a sort of nothingness?

PKF: I sincerely hope not. It was only after oral tales became written orthodoxies that some people were labeled "pagans" and "heretics" and burned at the stake for unorthodox views. The greatest strength media ecology possesses is its ability to generate unorthodox views. Media ecology makes a better "Trojan horse" than a golden bull.

LR: Finally, what are you currently working on and when is your next book coming out?

PKF: I am currently testing the limits of my inadequacy as editor of *EME: Explorations in Media Ecology*, the journal of the Media Ecology Association. I am working hard on it, but have the unenviable fate of following in the wake of the last editor, Corey Anton, a frighteningly intelligent guy and a fierce workaholic who did a fabulous job with EME over the last few years.

If I manage to survive this experience, I am very close to having prepared for publication what will be either a very lengthy biographical essay or a very brief book about a late-19th/

early-20th century Dublin barrister and amateur bibliographer, Ernest Reginald McClintock Dix. Dix represents, I believe, one of the last of the archetypal "men of letters" that McLuhan insisted were a natural by-product of alphabetic literacy.

I am working on a book on propaganda which seeks both to summarize all the research on that phenomenon to date and to update the work of Jacques Ellul to reflect the presence of newer, peer-to-peer digital technologies and social networks and their effects on the traditional "top-down," authoritarian information flows of pre-digital mass media.

I also claim to be working on a book, very much indebted to the thought of my teacher and mentor Christine Nystrom, about the possibility of human extinction as a result of our short-sighted and self-centered technological choices. I started it nearly three years ago and have made very little progress on it in the last few years. No, that's not true. I have made absolutely no progress on it in the last year. But I continue to claim that I am working on it. Perhaps you might ask me again this time next year?

My (Imaginary) Conversation with Marshall McLuhan

I had heard of Marshall McLuhan's *Understanding Media* as a freshman in high school in 1968, but didn't read it until four years later when I got to college. It was only the second book I had read about the power of media to shape societies (oddly enough for an eighteen-year-old, my baptism into the field of media studies was provided by Harold Innis's *The Bias of Communication*, but I had to read that one several times before I really, truly even began to comprehend it), and it so captured my attention and fired my curiosity that I was compelled to spend the rest of my life studying the interactions of technology and culture. So I was thrilled and proud when my first book, *Printing, Literacy and Education in Eighteenth Century Ireland: Why the Irish Speak English*, won the Media Ecology Association's Marshall McLuhan Award for Outstanding Book in the Field of Media Ecology in 2007.

Yet, since almost the very beginning I've been bothered by McLuhan. I was looking for answers and McLuhan kept posing me riddles. Alternately dazzlingly clear and maddeningly cryptic, so much of what he had to say left many people feeling uncomfortable and skeptical; others, wildly enthusiastic and hopeful. For me – and many others who were moved to dedicate their lives to understanding media – McLuhan's words were intriguing and enticing, inviting questions and urging deeper consideration. They made my head hurt, but they showed me for the first time that questions are, after all, far more important than answers.

I have, I believe, come to terms with McLuhan in the intervening thirty-eight years. Or I have almost come to terms with him. I'm at the very least minimally comfortable with his method; the "probe," oracular aphorisms, heuristic in nature, not particularly suited to empiric measurement, a kind of "intellectual Rorschach test" that everyone can read something into and get something out of.

What I am not comfortable with is a single phrase: "A moral point of view is a poor substitute for understanding in technical matters." So I decided to sit and talk with him about it.

What follows is a (totally imaginary) conversation I had recently with the "the oracle of the electric age." Many of McLuhan's responses are direct quotes from his works, many more are close paraphrases altered only for the sake of the literary integrity (such as there may or may not be) of this essay. I have, by necessity, invented some of McLuhan's responses to my questions posed here, but only then on the basis of what I honestly believe might have been his actual response. Needless to say, this essay very probably says more about me and my understanding of McLuhan than it does about McLuhan himself. But I'd be willing to argue that point:

Peter K. Fallon: "A moral point of view is a poor substitute for understanding in technical matters." Why? It seems to me that understanding technical matters absent a moral point of view is not "understanding" at all.

Marshall McLuhan: Well, first of all let me just mention that I don't always agree with everything I say. The point is not to say something and stand by it; the point is to push the limits of human perceptions and assumptions and see what we can find beyond them. If you don't like that idea, let's try something else. But you're right in asserting that my main theme has always been the extension of the nervous system in the electric age, and thus, the complete break with five thousand years of mechanical technology. This I state over and over again. And, no, I do not say whether it is a good or bad thing. To do so would be meaningless and arrogant.

PKF: And necessary. Because it seems to me that you're

abdicating moral responsibility for questioning the role of media in producing these changes in our nervous system. It seems to me that you're presenting as a given certain, almost pre-determined, consequences of technology and positing that this vague concept of "understanding" is all human beings can do in the face of rapid and radical technological change.

MM: Does that bother you?

PKF: Yes, it bothers me. It bothers me something awful. I have spent years defending you – from many who I don't believe really understand what you're saying – against the charges of "technological determinism," yet in far too many cases you sound as though you're saying that the best we can hope for is to understand the changes that technology brings us, not manage them.

MM: What does it matter if some call me a "technological determinist" or a "guru" or, for that matter, a "Charlatan"? There is absolutely no determinism in my work, because I urge a willingness to contemplate what is happening. I need no defense, Peter, from such charges. My job, as I see it, is to alert people to the changes going on around them. That in itself is a moral imperative, and no abdication of responsibility. Everybody experiences far more than he understands. Yet it is experience, rather than understanding, that influences behavior. I've just tried to bring more understanding into the picture. The electronic age has presented us with a dilemma: we are awash in electronic and digital information, and the swirl of this maelstrom of information tosses us about like corks on a stormy sea. But if we keep our cool during our "descent into the maelstrom," and study the process as it happens, like Poe's sailor we can save ourselves.

PKF: Yes. That's another thing. It's always bothered me that the "old sailor" – who was, of course, not old at all but aged prematurely by his ordeal – did not or could not save his brothers. One brother is flung outright from the boat, another goes mad at the sight of the enormous whirlpool and dies in its vortex. But the "old sailor" "keeps his cool" as you say and studies the patterns of the maelstrom. He notices – in a way that presages Einstein and relativity – that in the midst of the maelstrom's power, with its force propelling the boat in circles within its cone, he appears to be sitting still, and the opposite side of the whirlpool remains stationary in relation to him.

MM: Moving along within the maelstrom, at its speed, in its direction, there is a certain curious peace, and the sailor has time to study its patterns and make inferences about its behavior.

PKF: Yes, and he saves himself with the knowledge he gains within the chaos. But his brothers die.

MM: Well, yes. But, Peter, it's only a story. No one actually died in its telling by Edgar Poe.

PKF: But it's a story that describes your views on understanding media, that you have stated serves as a metaphor for your approach to studying media and their effects. And so we're back to my original difficulty: the idea of understanding anything absent a moral point of view. Why didn't he try to save his brothers?

MM: Because he would have died, it's as simple as that. Why is what you call "a moral point of view" so important to you, Peter? Is a "moral point of view," by its nature, any better or worse than an immoral point of view, or an amoral point of view, or a secular point of view, or a humanist point of view? Point of view, whatever its orientation, is imaginary. It is part and parcel of the typographic mindset, the cordoning off of the individual from the group, the artificial separation of one from the other. We don't live in that world anymore, but in a world of electric simultaneity that brings people together in a tribal village that is a rich and creative mix, where there is actually more room for creative diversity than within the homogenized mass urban society of Western man. In such a world a point of view – any point of view – reveals itself to be a dangerous luxury, an intellectual self-indulgence, especially when substituted for insight and understanding. You can believe that I need to take on a specific point of view – the scholar's point of view, the literary point of view, the cultural critic's point of view – but these are just self-indulgent affectations that obscure reality and true understanding. Mud sometimes gives the illusion of depth. But it's still mud.

PKF: But this "world of electric simultaneity" is a world of chaos and – to use Harry Frankfurt's term – bullshit, if you ask me. A world with no point of view and no real knowledge. And the fish can't experience the fishbowl. Isn't it someone's responsibility to make them aware beyond mere "understanding"? "Understanding media" today means the opposite of what you probably intended – or perhaps not...? "Understanding media" means knowing how to work them, knowing how to use them. Literacy has given way to "media literacy" and "information literacy" and "visual literacy" and point of view has given way to pointlessness and objectivity has given way to a truly egoistic subjectivity...I see no "rich and creative mix" – although people tell me I'm constantly surrounded by it – any more than I see understanding. And I don't see understanding any more than I see a moral point of view. We're left with nothing except a sort of psychic "I got mine, fuck you" environment that empowers us (if that is at all the appropriate word) to focus on ourselves to the detriment of the rest of the world. It seems to me that in a world like this, a point of view – if it is a positive point of view – is a Godsend. But what is worse, any point of view – even an entirely stupid one – strikes many who have none of their own, and are entirely unable to identify one, as a Godsend.

MM: Peter, you may be over-reacting. This age we live in of infinite connections and the liberation of consciousness from the body – the age of "discarnate man" – is barely half a century old. Innumerable confusions and a feeling of despair such as those you appear to feel invariably emerge in periods of great technological and cultural transition. Your assumptions about alphabetic man, if you'll allow me to say to you critically, may have outlived their uselessness. It was alphabetic man himself who was disposed to desacralize his mode of being, not we. In this electronic age we see ourselves being translated more and more into the form of information, moving toward the technological extension of consciousness, a seamless web of experience. This is not the individualist, trivial (in all senses of the word) consciousness of alphabetic man, but a consciousness that begins in the senses, is rooted in perception, and is derailed by concepts or ideas.

PKF: I know you're referring now, however obliquely, to your Christian faith, and specifically to your adopted faith of Catholicism.

MM: As you say.

PKF: And here again I have a hard time coming to terms with your ideas, which to my ears sound so sanguine. I know that your work was profoundly influenced by that of Pierre Teilhard de Chardin.

MM: I am not in the slightest influenced by Fr. Teilhard's works, even though we may share areas of common interest.

PKF: As YOU say. But Teilhard famously anticipated many of your ideas and even your tone. And I am a great admirer of Teilhard's work, as I am of yours…

MM: (~~feigns satisfaction with an irrelevant opinion~~)

PKF: …and I hope – no, I pray – that Teilhard is correct about many of his ideas, but I fear he is wrong. Because in the final analysis I do in fact see a determinism in your work, but it is not a technological determinism. It is a determinism of faith and salvation. Teilhard's "noosphere" is merely an anticipation of your "global central nervous system." And Teilhard's conception of the "Omega point" – the parousia – sounds very much like your idea that "Psychic communal integration, made possible at last by the electronic media, could create the universality of consciousness foreseen by Dante when he predicted that men would continue as no more than broken fragments until they were unified into an inclusive consciousness. In a Christian sense, this is merely a new interpretation of the mystical body of Christ; and Christ, after all, is the ultimate extension of man." You appear to have adopted an eschatological approach to your pursuit of understanding media – very, very similar to Teilhard's – that you don't ever explicitly identify.

MM: Is that so?

PKF: Well, I certainly believe it is so. It seems to me that you've put your faith entirely in acceptance of Christ – medium and message – without ever considering the human agency involved in salvation. As a Catholic, and in the knowledge of your devout Catholicism, I'm confounded by what sounds to me like the Protestant principle of sola gratia – salvation by God's grace alone – ignoring the quintessential Catholic principle of salvation by grace and good works. Your "evangelism" – it seems to me – is more of the Lutheran or Reformation variety than of a fully- (and rightly-) formed Catholic one.

Understanding media alone will not bring about a better world (the Kingdom of God?), but ought to be the foundation of good works that may bring it about: constructing an environment of truly free-flowing and uninhibited information, to be sure, but also reaffirming and supporting the structures of thought that allow us to identify error and falsehood, and empowering us to label bullshit as bullshit, as Harry Frankfurt suggests. The global village, with its "rich and creative mix" full of "creative diversity" can be the

perfect venue to put bullshit on an equal footing with truth.
I see nothing in this situation that is either constructive or
Catholic.

MM: That is your point of view.

PKF: (~~sigh~~) Yes, it is. I'll stand by it.

MM: In my defense, I'll say only this: The revealed and
divinely constituted fact of religion has nothing to do with
human opinion or human adherence. In Jesus Christ, there
is no separation or distance between the medium and the
message; it is the one case where we can say that the medium
and the message are fully one and the same. To know Christ
– to truly know him – is to accept Him. My work has always
been consistent with this thought, even if my public utterances
have not. As a consequence of our new extensions we have
become irrevocably involved with, and responsible for, each
other. So whether you approve of my emphases or not, I can
repeat that there is no greater moral action – no greater "good
work" – than understanding media.

Peter, I consider this to have been a good argument. I'm
glad you didn't ruin it.

(At any rate, that's how I imagine the conversation going...)

Sacrament and Anti-sacrament: Some thoughts on the Media Criticism of Jacques Ellul and Pierre Teilhard de Chardin

The reader is immediately forgiven for asking either of these two inevitable questions: What does theology – and especially Christian theology – have to do with media criticism? And where does a media scholar get off writing about two theologians? These are both fair questions. Before getting to my main subject I'll try to address these questions.

Media studies and religion actually have a long history. As Neil Postman pointed out in his well-known 1986 book *Amusing Ourselves to Death*, the first recorded instance of media criticism comes from no higher authority than God Himself (or, as the case may be, Herself). It is not insignificant that the second of some ten commandments delivered the prohibition against creating and/or worshipping *graven images*; false gods the Lord knew would lead His people away from Him (or, as the case still may be, Her people away from Her). The Lord was savvy about the power – and ambiguity and subjective nature – of images to distract us from reality.

Harold Innis, in his influential book *The Bias of Communication*, explained how early communication technologies created and supported what he called "monopolies of knowledge" based on their relative bias toward either time or space. Time-biased media – those that store information more effectively than they transmit it – commonly support monopolies of knowledge associated with traditional knowledge – mythological, cultural, or religious knowledge

– because of the transcendent nature of the knowledge that the social institutions that benefit from this type of knowledge wish to preserve. The entire emphasis in time-biased cultures is preservation; preservation of unchanging, eternally true, and absolute knowledge. On the other hand space-biased media – those that transmit information more quickly and efficiently than they store it – usually support monopolies of knowledge that cluster around the changing nature of information: the commercial, military, and political institutions. In a time-biased culture, information is valued for its stabilizing effects; in a time-biased culture, information is valued for the strategic advantages it provides.

Elizabeth Eisenstein, in her ground-breaking study of printing and literacy in early modern Europe, *The Printing Press as an Agent of Change*, noted that one of the effects of the introduction and speedy spread of printing in Europe was the Protestant Reformation. Up until 1452 the Roman Catholic Church, it is fair to say, held a virtual monopoly of the knowledge circulating through "Christendom" – a monopoly based on the written word and manuscripts. Few people, other than the vowed religious and the medieval nobility, could read or write. Little writing was done other than monastic scribes who copied and preserved sacred scripture. After 1452 that all changed. The Holy Bible became, thanks to Johannes Gutenberg, the first printed book in the history of humankind. It eventually became the first classic work of literature of any kind to be translated into a vernacular and printed for a mass audience after Martin Luther, himself a child of newly growing print literacy, posted his 95 theses on the church door at Wittenburg. It is probably no coincidence that both Gutenberg and Luther were German; that both the printing press and the Reformation are fruits of the same garden. The space-biased printing press destroyed the monopoly of knowledge that had been held by the Church during a millennium of time-biased handwriting.

Media are *epistemologies*. Every medium implies a particular way of thinking about things, influences to great extent what things we will think about, and how we will think about them.

And so the importance of the study and critical analysis of mediated communication ought not to be considered only on its own, but in its relationship to other established areas of thought. Theology – what we believe about "God" and how we believe it – certainly deserves the same sort of attention that politics, economics, sports, and entertainment deserves.

Pere Pierre Marie Teilhard de Chardin and Jacques Ellul were two twentieth-century French Christian theologians who happened to integrate theories of mediated communication into their works. They did so in distinctly different ways, from distinctly different perspectives, for distinctly different reasons. It shouldn't surprise us that they came to distinctly different conclusions, each of which we should consider and understand, for each has implications for our ethical decision-making processes in a complex, highly-developed technological society.

Pierre Teilhard de Chardin was born in 1881, the fourth of eleven children, to a pious, provincial Catholic family in Auvergne, France. He entered the Jesuit novitiate at Aix-en-Provence in March of 1899, studying theology, geology, and paleontology, and was ordained into the Society of Jesus in August of 1911. He interrupted his studies during the First World War to serve as a stretcher bearer in the French Medic Corps (winning the *Croix de Guerre* in 1915), an experience of death and violence so profoundly disturbing that it forced Teilhard to confront and try to make meaning of some of the most confounding paradoxes of the human experience: the meaning of life and death, of violence in a universe created by a loving God, and the seeming incompatibility of science and faith. Could these things be explained? Understood? Could science and faith be reconciled?

After the war, he lectured in Science at the Jesuit College in Cairo, held a position as Professor of Geology at the Institute Catholique de Paris, and received his Doctorate in Paleontology from the Institute of Human Paleontology in Paris in 1922. Later that same year he went on an expedition in China where he was involved in the discovery and identification of the fossil remains of *Sinanthropus*, or "Peking Man," in 1929.

Teilhard's career was marked by ecclesiastical controversy. He saw what he believed to be an unfortunate and very artificial wall between science and theology; he wished desperately to knock that wall down. He believed in the presence of God in all creation, both spiritual and material. For Teilhard the scientist, the material world was a source of Divine mystery and wonder, providing a vision of God's loving providence; for Teilhard the theologian, the truth of a divinely-directed evolution was self-evident.

While in China, he put his thoughts on paper in what he called "a little book on piety": *The Divine Milieu*. In it, Teilhard stated his belief that the Divine permeates all of creation, that there is "a little bit of God," if you will, in every rock, every tree, every running stream. As these things seem to happen, a copy of the manuscript found its way to Rome, attracting the attention of ecclesiastical authorities at the Vatican. The reaction against Teilhard's "modernist" heresies was immediate and severe. He was removed from his teaching positions and instructed not to publish any of his observations on religion and science. A *monitum* was placed on his works, warning that they "abound in such ambiguities and indeed even serious errors, as to offend Catholic doctrine," effectively banning them "to protect the minds, particularly of the youth, against the dangers presented by the works of Fr. Teilhard de Chardin and of his followers." This monitum stands today.[1]

It was only after his death in 1955 that over a dozen of Teilhard's manuscripts, journal notes, diaries, and private letters – cannily given by Teilhard to a small group of Jesuit and lay friends – were edited and prepared for publication. Ostensibly the writings of a scientist, these works give eloquent witness to Teilhard's love of God and God's creation. Despite his protests to the contrary, and not surprisingly, they lack the rigor and objectivity that scientific method demands, and the consequent reaction of the established scientific community has been just as harsh as that of Rome. Yet Teilhard has found, in the last forty years, a solid and cult-like following among lay and religious Christians, some scientists, ecologists, and Internet aficionados.

Jacques Ellul was born on January 6, 1912 in Bordeaux, France. Some sources claim a Catholic baptism[2] even though Ellul's father was a skeptic and "Voltairian"[3] and his mother a Protestant who didn't attend services according to her husband's wishes. Ellul himself states that his early years were not influenced by religion in any formal sense.[4]

As a young man Ellul was familiar with the docks and longshoremen of Bordeaux, with their labor and their lives. Ellul became an enthusiast of the writings of Karl Marx at age 19 (having already lapsed into a not-unexpected atheism in his early teenage years), and then at age 22 he converted to Reformed Christianity (he never, however, completely abandoned Marx or his ideas). Ellul fought with the French resistance during World War II and the National Liberation Movement in 1944.

Educated at the Universities of Bordeaux and Paris, he taught Sociology and the History of Law at the Universities of Montpelier and Strausbourg. In 1946 he returned to Bordeaux where he lived, wrote, served as Deputy Mayor, and taught until his death in 1994.

In his 40 books and hundreds of articles, Ellul's dominant theme has been the threat to human freedom – and to Christianity – posed by modern technology. In his sociological works, his tone is objective, his method scholarly and meticulous, his perspective a sociological one. Few of his books are overtly theological; several of his books, including *Propaganda: The Formation of Men's Attitudes* and *The Technological Society* are required reading in many mass communication curricula.

I came into contact with Teilhard and Ellul at different times in different ways. Thirty years ago, a (former) Jesuit friend of mine who knew of my academic interest in communication suggested that I read Teilhard's *The Phenomenon of Man* because of Teilhard's championing of what he called the *noosphere*. This friend saw the connection to the thought of Marshall McLuhan and thought I would be intrigued by Teilhard. Indeed, Teilhard's ideas sounded more than a bit McLuhanian (or vice versa), and the concept of the noosphere echoed McLuhan's claim that electronic communication networks were creating a "global central nervous system," making of the world a single collective organism.

I encountered Ellul only in graduate school, at first in a course on sociological propaganda. His views on the technologically-mediated world of our own creation were so at odds with Teilhard's that I was immediately intrigued. I went on to read *The Technological Society* and *The Technological Bluff* for some other classes, but it wasn't until many years later that, rummaging through new and used books in the old Barnes and Noble's 18th Street Annex in Manhattan, I came across a copy of *The Presence of the Kingdom*, Ellul's 1948 theological work about the place and role of the Christian in the technologically-developed world. Ellul the theologian – a respected and world-renowned theologian – was a revelation to me. In retrospect, however, I realize that there had always been in even Ellul's most overtly secular work a dual theme, subtly stated; a yin and yang of life in a highly developed technological society: sin and sacrament.

The things in these two lives held in common – the cultural milieu, the experience of war, the 20th century – contrasted against their almost entirely contradictory perspectives, provide a compelling reason to examine their ideas more closely, particularly those that deal with technologies of communication.

I've chosen five concepts common in the works of both men to contrast their approaches; I'm hopeful that these points will throw light on their opposing theologies, if you will, of communication. They are 1] evolution, 2] progress, 3] technology, 4] man, and 5] God. These themes are present in the works of each man – although they do not necessarily appear under the labels I've given them – and their perspectives on these themes are consistently opposed. It is instructive to look closely at each point and to consider what Teilhard and Ellul has to say about them.

1] Evolution. Teilhard, forbidden by the Vatican to write or teach on any issue which could be construed as theological, nonetheless constructed a model of creation and evolution that is profoundly reverential and God-centered, even as he attempted to maintain a façade of scientific objectivity and detachment. For Teilhard, evolution is a Divinely-directed process. There is indeed a power, an intelligence, which drives and directs evolution toward a pre-ordained end. There are no accidents in Teilhard's view of evolution; or, at the very least, what appear to humans as accidents are in fact inevitabilities pre-programmed – by God – into the process.

The origin of the cosmos, the moment of creation (what science now considers within the framework of "the big bang"), Teilhard calls "the Alpha point." Throughout the process of evolution, Teilhard tells us, there is a progression of states of being. This progression is marked by combining matter in aggregations of ever-increasing complexity and "interiorization." The aggregates themselves, and the tendency for matter to combine in such ways, are the result of cosmic (we may read "Divine") intelligence. These combinations of matter creating new, more complex, and more interiorized forms of matter are limited, however, by the relative complexity of each form. Each new form manifests some outer "face" consistent with its material makeup, but each also encloses some "inner" state of being, a proto-consciousness, which both directs and limits its material development.

These limits are defined by either environmental influences or by a heightened interior "drive" that pushes the form forward as a result of a mutually beneficial synergy with that environment. At the moment these limitations are reached, three possibilities present themselves for the form:

1. extinction;

2. stasis (having reached the limitations of its interiority, the mineral, for example, remains a mineral);

3. evolution to a higher form of complexity and consciousness.

This progressive process explains the propensity of electrons combining to form atoms, of atoms to become molecules, of elemental molecules to become compounds, of inorganic compounds to become organic, of organic compounds to become organisms, or *life*.

The evolution of life follows the same path so that some of the simplest organisms, directed by an ineluctable drive to develop, to grow to the limits of their consciousness, become, if and when the opportunity arises, more complex and more conscious.

The appearance of man on Earth, according to Teilhard, marks the end of biological evolution. Man is different, he says, and he is different in a way which can neither be accidental or unanticipated. Man is the first and only creature in the universe to have a consciousness so highly developed that it is *self*-conscious. "Man discovers," Teilhard tells us, "That he is nothing else than evolution become conscious of itself."[5] From this point forward, evolution continues not as a biological phenomenon, but as a phenomenon of consciousness, of intellect, of *spirit*.

This evolution of the *within* of man will continue until there is true unity of spirit. Directed by interior *energies* which compel being both to unite and to move forward, the phenomenon of man will culminate in, to use Teilhard's colorful phrase, "a paroxysm of harmonized complexity."[6] This will be the end times spoken of in the Bible, what Teilhard calls the "Christification of the universe," the pleroma, the Omega point. All of creation and all of evolution is a directed and pre-determined journey from Alpha to Omega.

Ellul, on the other hand, will have none of this.

Ellul's education, training, and experience as a sociologist does not allow him to look upon anything like a "phenomenon of man" except in the most narrow of views, the *here and now*. He will not consider evolution as a directed process or man having a pre-determined fate. Rather, he looks at the human situation as it exists *now*, to evaluate it in its current condition. He rejects the notion of Divine direction in human affairs or pre-determinism in evolution. To Ellul, history (and, by extension, evolution) is a *dialectical* process. History, he says, is open and the way before us is ambiguous. The particular future that lies before us is not determined for us, but dependent *on* us; on the choices human beings make among a number of possibilities we can't see clearly leading us in directions we don't necessarily know.

Recognizing this, however, it is also important to note that Ellul has written that he sees a distinct directionality to the course of human affairs, and the body of his work gives an indication of where he thinks we're going. And it isn't pretty. Human history is the story of series after series of tragic mistakes made on the basis of equally tragic choices. Ellul, fairly or unfairly, has been called deterministic (a characterization he rejects), even fatalistic in his view of human history and the future of humanity. But he acknowledges that human beings have it in their power to choose their course, to determine and direct their own future, if only they will make the difficult choices – and make them correctly.

> (If) man – if each one of us – abdicates his responsibilities with regard to values; if each one of us limits himself to leading a trivial existence in a technological civilization, with greater adaptation and increasing success as his sole objectives; if we do not even consider the possibility of making a stand against these determinants, then everything will happen as I have described it, and the determinants will be transformed into inevitabilities... Fatalism is not involved; it is rather a question of probability, and I have indicated what I think to be its most likely development.[7]

2] Progress. Teilhard looked upon evolution as a Divinely-directed process with a clear and unambiguous direction whose fulfillment is the fulfillment of all creation. The idea of progress, therefore, is implicit in his work, and Teilhard's faith in the idea of progress is a function of his overall Christian faith. But ever the scientist, he also cites biology to justify progress as a powerful determinant of evolution. The (now largely discredited) theory of recapitulation – summed up in Ernst Haeckel's phrase "ontogeny recapitulates phylogeny" – suggests for Teilhard a law of irreversibility in evolution. Since, he tells us, "a being stores traces of each phase that it goes through, it is incapable, by construction, of returning exactly to any of the states through which it has passed."[8]

As we noted earlier, Teilhard considered biological evolution to have ended with the emergence of oh human beings. But the process of evolution goes on, he says, and must continue to do so in a way that reflects the principle of progress. Interior energies impel us toward unity of consciousness. "Life moves toward unification,"[9] and it is man's complex consciousness which promises this progressive movement. What is the end of progress? Fulfillment of man's – and the universe's – evolution: The Omega point. Humankind will achieve a collective consciousness, our "interior" knowledge, that cosmic or Divine knowledge, will become exteriorized by the same forces that have impelled evolution since creation, and mankind will complete its evolutionary progress in its ultimate and highest form: the unified and universal body of Christ.

For Ellul, however, progress is simply another human myth, as tantalizing in its promise as it is cataclysmic in its fulfillment; a dangerous fantasy which needs to be openly rejected:

> I refuse to believe in the 'progress' of humanity, when I see from year to year the lowering of standards among men I know, whose lives I follow, in the midst of whom I live – when I see how they lose their sense of responsibility, their seriousness in work, their recognition of a true authority, their desire for a decent life – when I see them weighed down by anxiety about what the great ones of the world are plotting, by the fear that penetrates our world, by the hatred which they feel for a terrible phantom which they cannot even name; when I see them cornered by circumstances, and, as they suffer, becoming thieves and frauds, embittered, avaricious, selfish, unbelieving, full of resistance and rancor; or when I see them engaged in a desperate struggle, which comes from the depths of their being, against something they do not know.[10]

Secondly, Ellul suggests that rather than progressing along

a road which will lead us inexorably toward some mystical "Omega point," a state of being marked by universal good will and a global consciousness imbued with Divine love, man has created for himself, by consistently choosing the worldly over the Divine, a culture of death, and Ellul sees no evidence that we are willing to change our collective direction:

> Our whole civilization needs to be examined, and by each person, on the plane of his individual destiny, which may not be heroic, but which is certainly a human destiny, and cannot exist without genuine communication with the human beings who surround him.
>
> Here we ... come upon one of the characteristics of our day: the "will-to-death," one of the forms of universal suicide toward which Satan is gradually leading man. Satan makes people gradually get used to this idea of suicide: suicide in enjoyment or despair, intellectual or moral suicide, and thus people are ready for the total suicide which is slowly preparing, and will involve the whole world, body and soul.[11]

Thirdly, Ellul believes that the idea of progress, and particularly that of technological progress, is fundamentally illusory, transient, and a distraction from reality – a fatal distraction from truth. "Progress" as a social concept has become an end in itself, rather than the means to some greater end.

> Everybody today is aware of the general aim of civilization, and it seems futile and old-fashioned to ask questions about it. Everybody has vague ideas about "progress," and it seems that this notion of progress might be capable of replacing the pursuit of ends. People think that whenever there is change there is progress...[12]

The differences of opinion about human progress that we see in Teilhard's and Ellul's writings demand that we turn our attention to another discussion, one of a concept which is critical to our understanding of these two thinkers: the idea of technology's place in the history of humankind.

3] Technology. It is not at all surprising – but still necessary to point out – that Teilhard sees all technological change ("progress") as a natural consequence of human intelligence, and an inevitable part of human evolution. Human technologies are not "artificial," but natural phenomena created by a being who partakes in a very high level of cosmic (i.e., Divine) consciousness. We may legitimately infer from this, I think, that Teilhard would agree that God's work on Earth is man's work, as man is God's worker. God gave human beings the intelligence to create solutions to problems, and it is an abdication of a lofty responsibility to distance oneself from the man-made in favor of the natural.

> ...(Is) it not precisely the world itself which, culminating in thought, expects us to think out again the instinctive impulses of nature so as to perfect them? Reflective substance requires reflective treatment... We need and are irresistibly being led to create, by means of and beyond all physics, *a science of human energetics*.[13]

The technologies human beings create are marked by a sort of moral neutrality. The significance of any technology is not what we *might* do with it, but what we *actually* do with it. And what we actually do with a technology is largely dependent on what it allows us to do – or forces us to do. So rather than viewing the splitting of the atom, the explosive release of nuclear energy, and the creation of an atomic bomb as singularly catastrophic events in human evolution, Teilhard instead seeks out the positive. The nuclear age, while beginning as one of tension, fear, and anxiety, or implied and expressed threats, and of the obliteration of hundreds of thousands of human beings, has forced human beings to step back from the brink of confrontation and to seek compromise and entente. "The atomic age," Teilhard tells us, "is not the age of destruction, but of union in research."[14] Because it acts to further focus man's consciousness upon himself, technology, Teilhard suggests, must act as an agent of progress: "Peace...is certain: it is only a matter of time. Inevitably, with an inevitability which is nothing but the supreme expression of liberty, we are moving laboriously and self-critically towards it."[15]

What makes Teilhard's stance on technology particularly interesting from the point of view of media and communication scholarship is his belief that technological progress is central to the culmination of human evolution. If mankind is to unite into some kind of "super-body," the indivisible body of Christ, then communication technologies must be at the center of this transformation. Let's consider why this must be so from Teilhard's unique perspective.

The evolution of matter, as Teilhard explained it, brought us to an eventual and inevitable point where enormous bodies of chemical compounds, minerals, and elements followed a mutual attraction and formed *baryspheres*: nascent planets. Some planets, such as Earth, formed a *hydrosphere* of hydrogen and oxygen – necessary for life – and an *atmosphere*. All these factors create the possibility of (and will eventually nourish) a *biosphere*, the envelopment of the planet in *life*. With human beings the final phase in evolution begins, with a new layer slowly blanketing the Earth, a layer of thought, a layer of intelligence, a layer of consciousness: the *noosphere*. As mankind evolved, humans created new techniques and technologies which helped to spread this layer of consciousness. The various technical apparatus of communication constitutes "a machine which creates, helping to assemble, and to concentrate in the form of an ever more deeply penetrating organism, all the reflective elements upon earth."[16] Teilhard saw radio and television as media promising the "direct inter-communication of brains" which "link us all in a sort of 'etherized consciousness.'"[17] Computers promise to move information at the "speed of thought."[18] Even though Teilhard didn't live to see the era of global satellite and telecommunication network technologies, he anticipates the magnitude of their potential, and is widely credited in cyber circles for creating, in his *noosphere*, the conceptual foundation for the Internet. "What Teilhard was saying here can be summed up in a few words," notes cyber-guru John Perry Barlow. "The point of all evolution up to this stage is the creation of a collective organism of Mind."[19]

Not surprisingly, Ellul disagrees. "An expression that caused great excitement was that television was changing our world into a small village. I do not accept that."[20] He sees technology as nothing less than the instrument of human self-destruction. He believes that we have created for ourselves a "technological society," an entirely artificial reality which is predicated upon the all-encompassing values of efficiency, convenience, productivity, speed, progress, etc., and to which we are totally subjected and subjugated. "Let no one say that man is the agent of technical progress…and that it is he who chooses among possible techniques… He can decide only in favor of the technique that gives the maximum efficiency. But this is not his choice."[21] "(The) human being must be completely subjected to an omnipotent technique, and all his acts and thoughts must be the objects of the human techniques."[22] But going even further, Ellul turns Teilhard's entire concept of *Christification* on its head, portraying the unity Teilhard envisions as an even greater threat to human freedom. "When psychological techniques, in close cooperation with material techniques, have at last succeeded in creating unity, all possible diversity will have disappeared and the human race will have become a bloc of complete and irrational solidarity."[23]

Technology, once mere tools used to extend human capabilities through time and space, now become the instruments of enslavement and suicide.

From this perspective, technology certainly appears to be a behavioral determinant, inconsistent with the Christian concept of free will. But Ellul – Marxist enthusiast and Christian theologian – embraces the paradox and disagrees with this criticism: "I don't believe in a permanent determinism, in the inexorable course of nature. Fate operates when people give up."[24] How is it, then, that technology creates such an environment for man that he is so ready, so willing, so able to "give up"?

First of all, as Ellul explains, technology creates a total environment which is antithetical to nature. It is no more possible (we might even say desirable) for modern man to avoid technology than it is for him to avoid breathing. In fact, it is much simpler for man to avoid himself (his thoughts, dreams, fear; his sense of the transcendent) than to avoid technology. In order to be comfortable in a milieu which is totally artificial and separated from nature, he must be constantly indoctrinated about the "rightness" and (paradoxically) the "naturalness" of this totally artificial environment:

> When a society becomes increasingly totalitarian (and I say "society" and not "state"), it creates more and more difficulties of adaptation and requires its citizens to be conformist in the same degree. Thus, this technique becomes all the more necessary. I have no doubt that it makes men better balanced and "happier." And there is the danger. It makes men happy in a milieu that normally would have made them unhappy, if they had not been worked on, molded, and formed for just that milieu. What looks like the apex of humanism is in fact the pinnacle of human submission...[25]

Secondly, technology destroys *ends* as we know them. While giving lip service to high-flung concepts as "the greater good of man" or "the pursuit of happiness," the technological means do not directly affect these abstract ends, or even "man" in the abstract, but affect flesh-and-blood man, without regard to his greater good or happiness. Flesh-and-blood man, therefore, in accepting his subservience to "man in the abstract," becomes (willingly or unwillingly) part of the means to an end that exists *only* in the abstract. "In reality, today what justifies the means is the means itself, for in our day everything that 'succeeds,' everything that is effective, everything in itself 'efficient,' is justified."[26]

It is easy to appreciate, in a world where flesh-and-blood man is reduced to the level of mere means at the service of "man in the abstract," that respect for the lives of those who are not "useful" (the elderly, the poor, the physically or mentally disabled, the undesirable) is not a high priority. By creating a world in which efficiency and utility are the measure of value, technology destroys the critical sense:

> (Means) have become so exclusive that they exclude everything that does not help their progress, everything that is not suitable for their development. On the one hand, then, the means destroys all that threaten its development: thus technics will attack and ruin successively the moral judgment (and in consequence morality as a whole); the humanism which claims to subordinate all things to man (but technics does not admit that it can be limited by the interests of man); all the activity in which man expresses himself freely for the disinterested pleasure in the activity itself, for everything must be "useful" ... and all spiritual awareness (because it is essential that man should be blind, in order that he may be a good slave of the means he creates). Technics will abolish the critical sense, in order to be able to develop freely (as everyone thinks) for the greater good of humanity.[27]

Technology, in such a society, is *always* justified because it frees us from choice, thus making life easier.

Thirdly, and perhaps most significant in its relation to our overall comparison, Ellul tells us that technology destroys human communication. Communication technologies make available to man more and more pieces of information of various types, but the individual bits of information have, by and large, nothing to do with man's life.

> (Every day) he himself has a number – a very limited number perhaps – of genuine experiences, but he is so embedded in his habits that he doesn't even know it! On the other hand, every day he learns a thousand things from his newspaper and his radio – and very important, very sensational things. Can he help it, that his little personal experiences – which deal, perhaps, with the excellence of a plum or the condition of a razor blade – are drowned in this flood of important illusions concerning the atom

bomb, the fate of Germany, strikes, and the like? Now these are facts of which he will never know the reality.[28]

Our contemporaries only see the presentations that are given them by the press, the radio, propaganda, and publicity. The man of the present day does not believe in his own experiences, in his own judgment, in his own thought: he leaves all that to what he sees in print or hears on the radio. In his eyes, a fact becomes true when he has read an account of it in the paper... What he has himself seen does not count, if it has not been officially interpreted, if there is not a crowd of people who share his opinion.[29]

This fundamental separation from his own individual intellect is one of the factors which makes it so easy for man to "give up," for he himself – we ourselves – have no idea of the meaning of life. We have no sense of the transcendent, only of the here-and-now "facts" of our artificial technological society, and "if God is no longer regarded as true in our day it is because he does not seem to be a fact."[30]

Technologies also destroy human communication as a result of their need to integrate man into the technological society. They do this by fascinating man, amusing him, and distracting him from the essentially artificial and alienating nature of modern life.

Today everyone is "distracted" by civilization; indeed, we might say that our whole civilization, from its games and sports up to serious business, has arranged everything in order to achieve this distraction... (Man's) way of life, his amusements, his work, his political parties, etc. – all this absorbs modern man to such an extent that he easily falls prey to these ways of acquiring information. Their influence is strengthened by the man who uses them, who is profoundly incapable of meditation and reflection.[31]

Television is one of the chief forces that exercises fascination in our society... Its power to fascinate is much greater than that of the cinema. We may also quote the hours spent in watching it (4 hours a day on average in France, 7 hours in the USA). These figures give us some idea of its influence on ideas, opinions, and political orientation. On this level television has much more power than any other medium. It affects the psyche and the personality...[32]

(Television) has no message apart from itself. It does not transmit anything, whether information, thought, or artistic creation. It is itself the message. What it implants in us as message is itself. The pictures that it presents have no meaning. This is why they must be short and striking. Dancing is more televisual than yoga, a papal visit than meditation, war than peace, violence than nonviolence, the shouting of a charismatic leader than reflection that expresses ideas, conflict and competition than cooperation. Ecology does not go over well on television. Non-messages go over best. All that remains is a general haze out of which only the screen itself emerges. We are given no information about reality.[33]

Ellul's analysis of technology and its evolution leads him to the stark conclusion that human beings have created a nightmare reality through which they sleepwalk unconsciously: a world without human communication. In such a world, he asks us, what is the meaning of Christianity?

4] Man. From all that we have seen so far in Teilhard's work, we can infer the following fundamental assumptions about the human person: we represent the highest point in biological evolution; we hold the promise of further evolution on the spiritual or intellectual plane; we represent the phase of evolution responsible for the creation of the noosphere, instrumental in the exteriorization of cosmic (Divine) intelligence which resides within us; and that we ourselves will be instrumental in the creation of the Omega point, the Christification of the Universe.

But in man we confront, for the first time in evolution, the problem of sin. Teilhard suggests to us that it is *unconsciousness* – what I interpret in his work as a failure to be fully present to our world – that is the foundation of sin. This is the sin that results from our failure to share in the creation and fulfillment of the universal body of Christ, and all the benefits that flow from it. This sin, along with the sins of solitude and fear[34], which allows us to inhibit and avoid our own interior forces compelling us to unite, are the sins peculiar to man because they imply an active *turning away* from the collective reality of humanity. Other sins experienced and committed my human beings, such as disorder and failure, decomposition and chaos, and, significantly, the evil of growth, are systemic evils and a transitory part of the evolutionary process and resemble "nothing so much as a way of the Cross."[35] Ultimately, however, man's recognition of sin is an index of his ability to confront it and rectify it.

Once again, Teilhard's faith is matched by Ellul's skepticism. Man is far from being the paragon of creation, he says, not because he is not the most highly evolved creature, but because of all creatures, man is the one who has not lived to the limits of his potential, and has not done so because he has *chosen* not to do so.

Ellul the sociologist concludes that man, when he hasn't completely ignored – or allowed himself to be distracted from – the difficult choices he must make, has made consistently poor choices. And we continue to make them. Human beings abdicate responsibility for our own freedom, and by doing so are complicit in our enslavement. This is our sin. "Freedom is not static but dynamic; not a vested interest, but a prize continually to be won. The moment man stops and resigns himself, he becomes subject to determinism. He is most enslaved when he thinks he is comfortably settled in freedom."[36] Sin, for Ellul, consists in just such an abdication of responsibility and the consequent acquiescence to determinism.

5] God. Despite the fact that he was officially banned from theological writing, and indeed because his own Jesuit Order would not allow Teilhard to publish his thoughts (all of his books were published, as were many not-for-publication notes, journals, and letters, posthumously by his estate), we have very strong statements of Teilhard's belief in the centrality of God to the process of evolution. In the text of his "scientific" works (and at this point it is rather meaningless for me to pretend that I see Teilhard more as a scientist than a theologian unacceptable to the Church), he may speak about the interior proto-consciousness of matter, or of the *tangential* and *radial* energies that bind us together, but we can be fairly certain that he is speaking, respectively, of the Divine knowledge (logos) he believes to be at the center of all things, and of Divine love. "Christ is the instrument, the centre, the end of all animate and material creation' by Him all things are created, sanctified, made alive."[37] For, without God to give meaning to the cosmos, the planet, the struggle and growth of life, humanity's very existence is little more than a curious accident of the universe, a stone skipped across a vast cosmic lake which, once it has run its course and sunken into the dark depths of oblivion, will leave little more than a ripple in time to be seen by – no one.

Ellul agrees – to a point. His faith in God – if we judge him not only by his words but also his actions – is very strong indeed. Yet again he parts company with Teilhard in the essential point of view of his faith. Where Teilhard proclaims the inevitability of evolution, to the belief that man has a destiny to which God has pre-ordained him, Ellul prophesies that all will be lost and humankind doomed if we don't take action. "[If] we let ourselves drift along the stream of history, without knowing it, we shall have chosen the power of suicide, which is at the heart of the world."[38] The role of the Christian in modern life should be that of *revolutionary*: "This, then, is the revolutionary situation: to be revolutionary is to judge the world by its present state, by actual facts, in the name of a truth which does not yet exist (but which is coming) – and it is to do so because we believe this truth to be more genuine and more real than the reality which surrounds us. Consequently it means bringing the future into the present as an explosive force."[39]

God will not save us at the mast minute, Ellul is telling us, from *ourselves*. Nothing is pre-determined. Nothing is given.

Salvation is not automatic. We must be lulled into thinking that we can rest easily, assured of our own salvation. For being part of a systematic culture of death, unquestioning, acquiescent in its ascendancy, we are complicit in our own enslavement, and that of others. We must stop being merely means. "The whole object of ethics is not to attain an end…but to manifest the gift which has been given us, the gift of grace and peace, of love and of the Holy Spirit; that is, the very end pursued by God and miraculously present in us."[40]

And whereas Teilhard's eschatology is, in a sense, tied to his overall perspective of man in evolution (that is to say, a creature not yet fully developed, not yet capable of achieving Omega), Ellul insists that the eschaton is *now*. "The point from which we ought to start is that in the work of God the ends and the means are identical. Thus when Jesus Christ is present the Kingdom has 'come upon' us."[41] A rejection of the modern world, and all it entails and implies, coupled with a renewed commitment to living our lives as intelligent, transcendent, and immortal souls is the essence of revolutionary Christianity.

> It is the fact of living, with all its consequences, with all that it involves, which is the revolutionary act par excellence; at the same time this is the solution of the problem of the end and the means. In a civilization that has lost the meaning of life, the most useful thing a Christian can do is live – and life, understood from the point of view of faith, has an extraordinary explosive force.[42]

In considering these five points, it becomes clear that Teilhard and Ellul present us with a clear choice between two orientations toward each of the points, and two distinct courses of action we might consider for our lives. Do we live our lives in an imperfect world the best we can in the hope – a hope, we must in fairness admit, informed by a profound faith in an infinitely loving and merciful God – that God does indeed have a plan for all creation that we, at our present level of intellectual and spiritual development, are simply unable to understand? Or do we take greater responsibility for ourselves and our world and accept a more active role in creating the future, in forging our own destinies? Should we assume, like Voltaire's Dr. Pangloss, that all is for the best in this best of all possible worlds, and that time and progress – that mysterious and ineffable force of nature – will bring improvements to the human material and spiritual condition? Or should we recoil in horror and disgust from this world we have created (or are, at the very least, complicit in creating through our poor choices)? Do we live in a world where we see human beings reaching out to each other – especially through the agency of new communication technologies – sharing their love and laughter, their travails and tears? Or do we live in a world where we are becoming more and more isolated from one another and more and more alienated from ourselves? Do we live in a world of growing global communication? Or do we live in a world of growing global lunacy? Is everything changing? Is anything changing?

Are we, in fact, limited by this dichotomous "either/or" approach? Is there no hope of achieving a synthesis of these two widely divergent perspectives? I'm not sure. But I believe it is possible. Let me explain why.

Evidence can be found to support both points of view. While we might hate television (for instance), there is reason to believe that it has improved the world by opening a window through which we have more (and more meaningful) experiences. Henry Perkinson, in his book *Getting Better: Television and Moral Progress*, argues that it was largely due to television's coverage of the civil rights movement of the 1960s, in which we witnessed men and women being beaten with truncheons, knocked off their feet by fire hoses, and attacked by police dogs, that a change in public opinion took place which resulted in landmark legislation being passed protecting the rights of African-Americans. It was largely due to television's coverage of the war in Vietnam that public opinion shifted away from American involvement. It was largely due to television's coverage of the Watergate scandal that public opinion shifted drastically away from support for Richard Nixon's presidency and made the threat of impeachment a possibility.

The Internet, too, appears to hold great promise for opening up channels of communication among diverse peoples all across the globe. Peoples of all races, nationalities, faiths, ages, genders, and cultural traditions have a forum to express their opinions and beliefs to a potential world-wide audience. The Internet could be an instrument for the free exchange of ideas and information within a structured context of equality, i.e., a context where we have no physical differences. Couldn't this uninhibited sharing of experiences, knowledge, and information help to create, in Teilhard's words, a global consciousness? Isn't that, in fact, exactly what is happening?

But Ellul would say, "Look at what we've done to television! Look at what we're doing to the Internet!" The 1960s were the era of, if not television's infancy, its rebellious adolescence. It's safe to say that we'll never see another war covered on television the way the Vietnam war was covered. Since the 1980s, the major networks, in conjunction with the Department of Defense, have implemented new policies for the coverage of military conflicts which are characterized by tight control of information and dependence on Defense Department footage.

The loosening of standards under Mark Fowler's FCC Chairmanship – he redefined the concept of broadcasting in the "public interest" to reflect the free-market principle that what interests the public is in the public interest – has resulted in a proliferation of non-traditional news formats and programs that more resemble entertainment (distraction?) than journalism. In fact, we've coined a new term for this type of programming: *infotainment.*

And look at the Internet. For all its vast potential, what have we made of this global information commons? We have created the electronic equivalent of Times Square, an enormous array of digital arcades, shopping malls, intrusive (but flashy and entertaining) advertisements, singles bars, porn shops, and cyber-bordellos. We see – that is to say, we have a vision of – what the Internet can be. But at the moment, it is difficult to argue that the 'net is anything more or less than another instrument of distraction and fascination in the technological society.

Even the Internet's much-touted strength as a research tool is questionable. The question is not, by the way, whether the Internet makes more information available more easily to more people more quickly (More! More! More! More!) than ever before. Certainly it does. But it also creates a context for students in which research is (and *ought to be*) simple. And it's not; nor is it supposed to be. It also redefines the concept of "research" in a way that gives the impression that it is more about finding information than synthesizing new knowledge from old. Thinking – and thinking *critically* – is serious business and hard work, and if we're doing it right seriousness and difficulty are exactly what we should be experiencing. And isn't it possible that global information technologies will foster a conception of education that makes the finding and delivery of information the *sine qua non* of learning, and not the ability to process, critically analyze, and make meaning out of information?

I think about Ellul's prophetic warnings in this way: just as God has given us sacraments – visible signs of God's love for us which confer grace and help us to become closer to God, human beings have given themselves *anti-sacraments*. These anti-sacraments are acts which, by their very commission, symbolize and actualize our turning away from God, and which confer upon us, perhaps, a measure of *anti-grace*: a pride, hubris, or over-arching self-confidence which help us to avoid God and isolate ourselves from God's love. Our communication technologies, like all technologies which serve us by allowing us to do more things more quickly, more easily, and more efficiently (More! More! More! More!), necessarily put a distance between us and the world we claim to be experiencing. Such reality-distancing instruments seem to be more naturally a part of an anti-sacramental, rather than a sacramental world, and facilitate anti-sacramental, rather than sacramental attitudes, beliefs, and behaviors.

I promised an attempt at a synthesis of Teilhard's and Ellul's opposing perspectives. Now is the time. I confess I share Jacques Ellul's suspicions about the direction of our technological "progress." I share his profound disappointment with the society we have created, and with the uses to which we have put some of the most spectacular new communication technologies imaginable. I share his conviction that our nation, our culture, our world is more concerned with "bottom-line" values of efficiency, productivity, and economic expansion than with what I see as more human (and more Christian) values of sharing, ideas and resources, voicing concerns, expressing care and love: *real human communication.*

And yet…and yet…I can't help but believe that there is truth in the arguments of Father Teilhard. Or perhaps it is that I so want to believe. I believe, in a way not terribly unlike Teilhard, that we are moving in a direction, and that that movement is directed – in *some* way – by an intelligence incomprehensibly greater than ours. I believe we are an imperfect species, but through the grace of God we have the gift to bring ourselves to completion. That gift is our human intelligence, a gift that is nurtured and strengthened by our search for meaningful information, our search for truth. But, like Ellul, I find it difficult to be certain about any of this and, in fact, my understanding of human history convinces me we need to make our decisions more seriously, more conscientiously, and with an eye toward the future and not merely the immediate results.

There are so many caveats attached to Teilhard's ideas. Are we, in fact, looking for truth? Or are we looking for support for our prejudices? If I am correct in both my beliefs and my doubts then it becomes critical that we takes steps – all of us – to be sure that the information we seek and find and use is meaningful, and that our search is for truth, not fascination, amusement, distraction, or support for prejudice. And what this demands is that we be conscious, awake, and aware of the world, our *actual* world, and actively engaged in it. It also demands that we be conscious and awake to *ourselves and to one another*; our joys, sorrows, concerns, fears, and hopes. On this one point both Teilhard and Ellul agree. Neither unconsciousness nor distraction will help us. I believe, like Ellul, that we make our destiny, that the future is open, that we are responsible for our choices, and that there are no guarantees that God, in the last moments of the universe, will save us from ourselves. Like Teilhard, I believe and hope and pray that we are headed in the right direction, that the phenomenon of man is a meaningful one, and that God created us for a purpose which we will understand perfectly in the fullness of time.

But I *know* that how we get to our destination is every bit as important as the fact that we get there at all. What we need to do is to show that we are agreed upon our direction, to prove that human life, indeed, has meaning, and to prove that we are worthy of the purpose – whatever it might be – for which we were created.

Like Ellul, however, I'm not sure I expect this to happen any time soon.

ENDNOTES

1. Sacred Congregation of the Holy Office, *Warning Regarding the Writings of Father Teilhard de Chardin* , CatholicCulture.org, retrieved July 1, 2012. http://www.catholicculture.org/culture/library/view.cfm?id=3160&CFID=145273415&CFTOKEN=53080650

2. Cf., for instance, Ellul's author page at Goodreads.com: http://www.goodreads.com/author/show/59700.Jacques_Ellul; the back cover of the paperback edition of *The Technological Society* includes this blurb from a published review: "Jacques Ellul is a French sociologist, a Catholic layman active in the ecumenical movement, a leader of the French resistance in the war, and – one is tempted to add, after reading his book – a great man. Certainly he has written a magnificent book… – Paul Pickrel, *Harper's*"

3. Ellul, Jacques, *Perspectives on Our Age: Jacques Ellul Speaks on His Life and Work*, Willem Vanderburg, ed., p. 2.

4. Ibid.

5. Teilhard de Chardin, Pierre *The Phenomenon of Man* (New York: Harper and Row, 1959), p. 221

6. Ibid., p. 262.

7. Ellul, Jacques *The Technological Society* (New York: Vintage Books, 1964), pp. xxix-xxx.

8. Teilhard de Chardin, Pierre *The Vision of the Past*, translated

by J.M. Cohen (New York: Harper and Row, 1966), p. 49.

9. Teilhard de Chardin, Pierre *The Future of Man* translated by Norman Denny (New York: Harper and Row, 1964), p. 72.

10. Elul, Jacques *The Presence of the Kingdom* translated by Olive Wyon (Colorado Springs: Helmers and Howard, 1989), p. 99.

11. Ibid., p. 96.

12. Ibid., p. 53.

13. Teilhard (1959) op. cit., p. 283.

14. Teilhard (1964), op. cit., p. 147.

15. Ibid., p. 153.

16. Ibid., p. 167.

17. Ibid.

18. Ibid.

19. Quoted in Kreisberg, Jennifer Cobb, *A Globe, Clothing Itself with a Brain*, Wired Magazine, Issue 3.06, June 1995. Accessed electronically on July 24, 2012, from: http://www.wired.com/wired/archive/3.06/teilhard.html

20. Ellul, Jacques *The Technological Bluff*, translated by Geoffrey W. Bromiley (Grand Rapids, MI: William B. Eerdmans Publishing Company, 1990), p. 334.

21. Ellul (1964) op. cit., p. 80.

22. Ellul (1964) op. cit., p. 410.

23. Ibid.

24. Ellul, Jacques *In Season, Out Of Season*, translated by Lani Niles (New York: Harper & Row, 1982), p. 106.

25. Ellul (1964) op. cit., p. 348.

26. Ellul (1989) op. cit., p 57.

27. Ibid., p. 61.

28. Ellul (1989) op. cit., p. 83.

29. Ibid., p. 82.

30. Ibid., p. 27.

31. Ibid., p. 87.

32. Ellul (1990) op. cit., p. 332.

33. Ibid., p. 333.

34. Teilhard (1966) op. cit., p. 74.

35. Teilhard (1959) op. cit., p. 313.

36. Ellul (1964) op. cit., p. xxxiii.

37. Teilhard (1964) op. cit., p. 304.

38. Ellul (1989) op. cit. p. 31.

39. Ibid., p. 38.

40. Ibid., p. 67.

41. Ibid., p. 64.
42. Ibid., p. 77.

Media History: Why the Irish Speak English

The notion that there once was a Gaelic-Irish culture, separate and distinct from English culture, and for that matter, from the Anglo-Irish hybrid which is today called Irish culture, is problematic for many. Many do not realize that Ireland was once distinctly different than today, and that Irish culture was as distinct from Anglo-Saxon or Anglo-Irish culture as Chinese culture is from Zulu. Ireland, over many centuries, lost (to borrow the title of a recent book) a "culture war" with England, losing much of its ethnic identity along the way; losing its native language; losing the philosophical and institutional underpinnings of its social organization; losing much of its epic poetry and oral literature; and losing whatever nascent sense of nationhood a pre-literate society might have achieved in nearly 3000 years.

In the final analysis, Ireland lost this culture war because Elizabethan England was becoming a modern empire; the medieval English nation was growing, becoming more populous, wealthier, more technologically advanced, and better organized politically and militarily. Naturally, those most closely associated with a living Gaelic-Irish culture resisted the pressures that spread English culture and government in Ireland. In consequence, Ireland lost this culture war only when the English managed over time to break down Irish cultural barriers to English dominance.

My first book, Printing, Literacy, and Education in Eighteenth Century Ireland: Why the Irish Speak English, traced the spread of printing and literacy in Ireland during a crucial fifty-year period at the end of the eighteenth century.

It is not a history of a medium, the printing press, but rather a "media history," a social and cultural history focusing on the dynamics of change when new technologies are introduced into a society. As such, it raises certain insistent questions: 1) Why did printing come so late to Ireland? 2) Why did it spread so slowly over the space of two centuries? 3) Why did printing make such rapid gains in Ireland in the last fifty years of the eighteenth century? and 4) Why did print ultimately make English the primary language of Ireland?

I argue that the spread of printing was inhibited, and its eventual assimilation took the shape it did, because there were, from at least the time of Elizabeth until the eighteenth century, two distinct cultures, two distinct societies, two distinct peoples in Ireland.

Until the coming of Christianity Gaelic-Irish was wholly oral. As my research shows, in the face of a series of invasions which brought with them the new medium of writing and the new modalities of thought and action it facilitated, Gaelic Ireland remained stubbornly oral.[1] Like other oral cultures before and since, Gaelic-Irish oral culture had a life of its own without regard to the written or printed page. It made up the very stuff of Irish social life, underlay its social hierarchies, and shaped the Irish view of the world and of what was worth knowing. These traits are characteristic of orality, that mode of communication and thought entirely dependent upon the spoken word.

By contrast, the Norman armies that invaded Ireland in the twelfth century, and their Anglo-Norman and English descendants who consolidated the conquest, did so by using the organizational, administrative, and technological skills made possible by the widespread cultural assimilation of literacy.

While Ireland remained purely oral, it seemed to have developed a powerful resistance to external cultural influences, surviving and rebounding after three separate invasions. *Why the Irish Speak English* looks at the differences between orality and literacy to understand why the Gaelic-Irish felt compelled to cling to it even though it put them at such a disadvantage against the threat of military invasion and political dominance by a technologically advanced outsider.

The coming of Patrick and Christianity to Ireland brought something of a revolution in its wake. For Christianity, the religion of the Word, was, by the coming of Patrick, the religion of the written word. A complex and elaborate bureaucracy had grown up around the church of Rome, a by-product of its intercourse with the deteriorating empire, and authority was exercised not only by virtue of expertise in scripture, but through epistles, written orders, commissions, and proclamations.

The church which Patrick established in Ireland was episcopal and hierarchical, and a synod held before his death upheld the principle of episcopal authority. This was the structure and methodology of the Roman church. Set up parallel to and making use of the organizational technologies of the falling empire (e.g., the written Latin language, Roman roads, Roman administrative techniques, etc.), the Roman church was as much a model for an alien political organization as it was a path to salvation.

It is interesting, therefore, that the Roman system of episcopal organization did not long survive the era of Patrick. A system of organization with a much higher degree of cultural relevance for Gaelic Ireland became the skeletal structure of the Irish church — monasticism.

In many ways, the system of monasteries punctuating the Irish countryside mirrored the clan system, wherein sovereignty resided in an extended family group, each clan was self-sufficient and ruled by a single chief or ard-ri, and clan leaders generally were selected from a ruling dynasty.

Christian monasticism, too, replaced the Druidic cults by offering the Gaelic-Irish a worldview which was consistent with their values and beliefs. Christianity was assimilated into Gaelic-Ireland relatively quickly, easily, and painlessly.

The coming of Christianity, letters, and monastic education did not spell the end of the old order, only of a small part of it. While the druidic schools died out with the druidic cults, the oral schools of the brehons, file and seanchaid flourished.

And so, at the end of the sixth century we see an Ireland on the threshold between orality and literacy. Pagan lore was not quashed, but was itself integrated into a Christian idiom, to create a new Christian mythology and the beginnings of an authentic Gaelic-Irish literature. Monastic schools and the oral schools met and complemented one another; orality and literacy struck a balance. As Gerhard Herm put it: "the monks and the singers were not enemies but, on the contrary...they worked closely together."

In the tenth century came the Vikings. The Vikings did not so much invade Ireland as make a series of incursions, acts of trespass, and raids on it. In violating Irish shores throughout the century, the Scandinavians showed no motive beyond gaining wealth. The Vikings were, at heart, traders with a keen understanding of the importance of expanding markets and finding new goods to buy and sell.

To be sure, the Norse raiders were usually violent with the Irish, and piracy was a prime method of "underwriting" the Viking expeditions. But many of these ambitious foreigners remained on Irish shores, founded trading settlements that became the first Irish towns and eventually became assimilated into the Christian faith and Gaelic-Irish social life.

However, a third invasion, one to have the most profound consequences for Gaelic Ireland, occurred in August 1170. Henry II, the Norman king of England and grandson of William the Conqueror, acted on a papal bull issued by Adrian IV (ironically, history's only English pope) in dispatching to Ireland an invasion force under Richard de Clare, Earl of Pembroke, ostensibly to bring the wayward Irish church into conformity with Roman orthodoxy. Strongbow, as de Clare was known, landed a force of some 3,000 Norman knights and infantrymen near Waterford. They were met in battle by a contingent of ill-prepared Norse Irishmen. The men of Waterford – fighting with weapons in use since the days of their Viking ancestors' original raids, clad in leather coats, wielding axes or "claymores" (claidhe mor, or broad swords) – were no match for a modern, technologically advanced army of foot soldiers and archers armed with cross-bows, and flanked by mounted knights bearing lances, shields, heavy helmets, and coats of mail. Waterford fell in a day. By September of that year, the Normans held Dublin. This was a classic invasion of conquest, systematically planned and executed with ruthless efficiency. By the end of the twelfth century, three-quarters of the island was in Norman hands. The widespread literacy among the Norman invaders expedited the conquest, consolidation, and administration of the conquered lands. Gaelic-Irish orality facilitated little more than helplessness in the face of this systematic aggression.

Yet the same tradition of orality that kept Gaelic Ireland from uniting politically to confront aggression from without served to help maintain cultural cohesion within, for by the fourteenth century the conquerors had come to resemble the conquered. Gaelic culture in Ireland had reasserted itself, and the Norman Irish had become thoroughly Gaelicized – speaking the Irish language, patronizing the arts of the Aes Dana, inter-marrying with the Gaelic Irish, and putting their children in the secular schools of the oral tradition as well as the monastic schools of the literate culture. These latecomers became "more Irish than the Irish themselves," and their names, though Norman in origin, are to our ears among the most Irish of all: Burke, Butler, Desmond, de Lacy, Fitzgerald, Fitzwilliam, Fleming, Joyce, Powers, to name but a few.

Anglo-Norman cultural standards at first prevailed only within "the Pale," the area within a roughly forty-mile radius of Dublin. They later gained a hold on the plantations of loyal Protestant farmers in the midlands and Ulster.

It was in Dublin that printing was introduced to Ireland in 1550 – brought, naturally enough, by the English, who had first adopted the new technology in 1477, only 25 years after its development. The expansion of the realm under the Tudors showed the printed word to be an expedient and efficient aid in large-scale administration. The English in Ireland believed that, having done so at home, print would speed up and simplify routine communication, establish uniformity throughout the realm, and ensure continuity of commerce and administration during times of governmental change.[2]

An Irish printing industry was slow to develop, however, as so few people outside the Pale spoke, read, or wrote English (or Irish, for that matter). A succession of printers held the King's patent allowing them to remain in business in the sixteenth and seventeenth centuries, guaranteed the contracts to print royal proclamations, government reports, and other state papers, which were of little interest to the natives outside the Pale – and not particularly important to the English within. Little other literary activity took place during this time. There were few booksellers or other outlets for printed material even in Dublin, and very little printing outside of Dublin. Few Irish towns had printing presses before 1750.[3]

The seventeenth century was a time of great upheaval in Ireland outside the Pale. A Catholic uprising, undertaken ostensibly to support the moderate Charles I against a militant puritan parliament, was an utter failure, and the Catholic Irish, both Gaelic and Norman, suffered as a result. A puritan revolution in England, during which Charles was overthrown and beheaded, and Oliver Cromwell was proclaimed lord protector of an English commonwealth, brought more misery to Ireland. English forces under Cromwell exacted vengeance for Irish Catholic support of the late king, and further plantations were instituted, displacing more Irish.

The Restoration of the monarchy under Charles II led to the unthinkable: at Charles's death, his brother James II, a Roman Catholic, ascended to the throne. Again the English revolted, proclaiming William of Orange King of England, and setting off a war that saw Irish armies routed, and Gaelic-Irish leaders exiled. An era of repressive legislation followed.

Having stopped the armies of Ireland, the English now set out to crush the nation itself. The newly buttressed Protestant Parliament in Dublin passed laws designed to ensure the demise of Catholic Gaelic-Irish culture. This marks the beginning of the "Penal Era" in Ireland during which it became illegal to educate an Irish child in anything but a Protestant school with a Protestant schoolmaster. The legislation also banished all Catholic clergy from Ireland on pain of imprisonment or transportation and made it a treasonable offense for a banished priest to return; prohibited foreign education and the immigration of non-Irish Catholic priests; made it illegal for

Catholics to own firearms, to "harbor" priests, or be guardians of children; excluded Catholics from voting and from the practice of law; and made it illegal for Protestants to marry Catholics and created inducements for the sons of Catholics to convert to Protestantism.[4]

By the early eighteenth century, Gaelic Ireland was a thing of the past – not dead, but irrelevant. Its traditions and beliefs could do nothing for a people but impoverish and penalize those who held them. Religious and cultural apostasy became the norm. "Hedge Schools" – illegal Catholic schools, remnants of the past oral tradition – taught reading and writing in English, and many Catholics converted to the established church to keep what property and land they had.

By the middle of the eighteenth century, a growing middle class of Protestant landowners and Catholic and Protestant merchants profited by assimilating the ideals of the literate English culture. Not coincidentally, this period saw a relative explosion in the spread of printing in Ireland.

Printing is known to have been done in only seven Irish cities prior to the eighteenth century: Dublin (1550), Waterford (1555-although there is no evidence of further printing until 1643), Cork (1644), Kilkenny (1645), Drogheda (1671), Limerick (1690), and Belfast (1694). These were all relatively cosmopolitan areas, either within the Pale or with a sizable planted English population. The output of printed material was insignificant in some of them, as is the case of Kilkenny and Waterford, where, during the Catholic uprising, portable presses issued Catholic propaganda supporting Charles I, but no further printing was done until the eighteenth century.[5]

After 1750 the number of new presses in Ireland increased dramatically. Twenty-seven more cities adopted the press; nearly quadruple the number that had done so in the previous 200 years. Those cities were: Athlone (1779), Birr (1775), Carlow (1778), Carrick-onSuir (1792), Cashel (1770), Cavan (1790), Clonmel (1771), Coleraine (1794), Downpatrick (1754), Dundalk (1782), Dungannon (1797), Dun Laoghaire (1756), Ennis (1778), Galway (1754), Hillsborough (1786), Kinsale (1795), Loughrea (1766), Monaghan (1770), Mullingar

(1781), Newry (1764), Roscrea (1786), Sligo (1752), Strabane (1771), Tralee (1774), Tuam (1774), Wexford (1769), and Youghal (1770).[6]

These were not the cosmopolitan centers that Dublin, Belfast, and Cork were in the seventeenth century, nor were they within the Pale or under the political or military sway of the English there. Many of the new English-speaking areas were in the Gaelic-Irish heartland in the southwest and west – areas that had once been solidly Gaelic, oral, and Catholic.

Throughout the eighteenth century, though printing continued to spread across Ireland, little was printed in the Irish language. This is not surprising. The Irish language had always been an oral medium, and when literacy (and the economic and social benefits bestowed by it) finally seduced the Irish mind, English became dominant. James Phillips reminds us that "the printing of books in the Irish language was of no real import until the nineteenth century" – by which time English language dominated the Irish linguistic landscape.[7] It was then that Irish became the object of study of that group of young educated Protestants and Catholics who initiated the so-called Gaelic revival – a prime example of McLuhan's observation that we know a phenomenon is truly dead when we put it in a museum and study it.

How does this 200-year-old history relate to the study of communication in the twenty-first century? It is, perhaps, a cautionary tale, one from which today's student of communication can learn. We should be aware of the fact that each new technology, each new information environment, is a new epistemology. When we learn to see and think about things in new and different ways, we need to consider what older ways of seeing and thinking we will lose.

This is not a rallying cry for active resistance to technological change; if anything, the lessons learned in the story of Irish cultural resistance to print should illustrate the futility of entrenchment. "Luddism" is not the answer, even if the Luddites accurately foresaw social and economic consequences to the Industrial Revolution largely unanticipated by its promoters. The key is to investigate all possible aspects and avenues of change and to make educated guesses about the direction, intensity, and speed of that change. We must learn to direct the evolution of society and of social institutions rather than ignoring possible consequences and "playing catch-up," cleaning up the social, political, economic, and cultural messes large-scale technological change can create. We must learn to be aware of the demands communication technologies make on us, as well as what they can do for us.

Each new technology empowers us in some way. It allows us to do something we haven't done before or to do something in a different and presumably better way. The example of printing in eighteenth century Ireland illustrates this. No one would argue that their assimilation of English literacy has been anything but beneficial to the Irish (or deny that Irish literacy in English has greatly enriched the entire English-speaking world). The problem, in fact, was not printing per se but the printing press as an agent of what was perceived to be a hostile foreign power. It is reasonable to assume that, left to their own devices, the Irish would have assimilated print technology (and probably much sooner than they did), and that they might thereby have developed a literacy and literature strongly flavored by the oral tradition.

So we must never forget that the benefits afforded us by new technologies come at a price, be it economic, political, educational, or environmental. I believe that we can lose some very precious gifts in a changeover from one technique to the next. And we may find that, once the change is done, we are impotent to undo it.

ENDNOTES

1. Fallon, Peter K. *Empowerment and Impotence: The Clash of Cultures and Media of Communication in Eighteenth Century Ireland* (Ph.D. Dissertation, New York University, 1996).

2. Quinn, David *Printing as an Instrument of Government and Administration*, Proceedings of the Royal Irish Academy 49, Sec. C

(Dublin: Hodges, Figgis and Co., 1943), p. 46.

3. Dix, Ernest Reginald McClintock *Early Printing in a Munster Town: Ennis*, Journal of the Cork Histrorical and Archeological Society, 2nd series, 10 (Cork: Curry and Co., Ltd., 1904), p. 123.

4. Vesey, Francis *The Statutes at Large, Passed in the Parliament Held in Ireland: from the Third Year of Edward the Second, A.D. 1310, to the First Year of George the Third, A.D. 1761, Inclusive* (Dublin: Printed by Boulter Grierson, Printer to the King's Most Excellent Majesty, 1765), 3:243-512, 4:5-31.

5. Dix, Ernest Reginald McClintock *A List of Irish Towns and the Dates of Earliest Printing in Each*, 2nd edition (Dublin: Corrigan and Wilson, 1909), p. 8.

6. Dix, Ernest Reginald McClintock *Kilkenny Printing in the Eighteenth Century*, The Irish Book Lover 16 (January/February 1928), p. 6.

7. Phillips, James W. *A Bibliographical Inquiry into Printing and Bookselling in Dublin, from 1670 to 1800* (Ph.D. Dissertation, Trinity College, Dublin, 1952).

Ernest Reginald McClintock Dix: The Last "Man of Letters"[iv]

Ernest Reginald McClintock Dix is not, as the name of this roundtable suggests, a "founding father" of anything, let alone of Media Ecology. The phrase "founding father" connotes the first of a kind. Dix was far from being the first of his kind, or even an unusual kind. He is, rather, representative of a kind once common, and now all but gone. He stands as an example of the archetype of the "man of letters" which, as Marshall McLuhan suggests in *The Gutenberg Galaxy*, didn't emerge until the eighteenth century[1], a product of the printing press and the print-driven Enlightenment. If McLuhan is correct in his observation it is not unfair to assume that, once literacy begins to recede beyond our postmodern cultural horizon, the phenomenon of the "man of letters" will also disappear.

Ernest Reginald McClintock Dix was only one such example of a "man of letters," a man not uncommon, in fact, in his own time, but increasingly rare (if not entirely extinct) in an information environment of electricity and digital pulses.

[iv]This is an edited version of a summary presentation of research given at the annual convention of the *Media Ecology Association* on June 11, 2010 at the University of Maine Campus in Orono. The theme of the presentation was "Founding Figures in Media Ecology." This essay forms part of an expanded biographical essay yet to be published. E.R. McC. Dix has been a fascinating figure to me since I learned of his work in the late 1980s. Without his lifetime of amateur scholarship, I would have had a much more difficult time gathering the objective data that was necessary to write my dissertation, and eventually my first book, *Why the Irish Speak English*.

He was just one of a large class of educated, middle-class professionals in Ireland, England, and elsewhere in Europe who functioned as amateur bibliographers, librarians, philologists, folklorists, and collectors, and made enormous contributions to the scholarship on printing, literacy, and the history of the book in the eighteenth, nineteenth, and early twentieth centuries. His story serves, I think, as a fitting illustration of all such amateur scholars, unburdened by the artificial, institutional pressures of "professional" scholarship. In his entire life Dix never labored under the imperative of "publish or perish"; yet he published nearly 150 journal articles, pamphlets, and books in the last four decades of his life, a number that would make most present-day academics dizzy. If that were not enough to seal one's legacy, he also endowed the National Library of Ireland with the most significant collection of rare, early Irish-printed books in the world – the Dix Collection – and all on a solicitor's salary. "Like a good many able Irishmen," one of Dix's American friends said, "his avocation was his real profession."[2]

In an "age of information," an Internet age of instant access to information, a "digital revolution," the age of Google and Wikipedia and scores of on-line databases, indices, and search engines, it is instructive to see the type of scholarship – all amateur – that the information environment of a century ago facilitated. It is also important to note and to think about, for those of us who are privileged to use research libraries and archives, just how much information is *not* available in the digital information environment, how much remains to be digitized, and whether it will ever be available in anything but hard-copy form.

I first encountered Dix and his work in 1990 while doing research in Dublin for a little book I was writing about the spread of printing and literacy in eighteenth century Ireland.[3] My thesis was that certain cultural, political, and linguistic circumstances impeded the rapid spread of printing there, unlike the rest of Europe. My research questions included investigating why it took a century after the development of movable-type printing for the first press to be established in Ireland, why in the next two centuries print technology made few inroads in Irish towns and cities, and why, in the last fifty years of the eighteenth century, there was a virtual explosion of printing across that green and fertile land – nearly all of it in the English language. Many of the canonical texts of Media Ecology helped me to frame the cultural, political, and linguistic arguments supporting my thesis, but I was left in something of a quandary regarding the objective data that I needed to give evidence of the slow spread of print technology. Was there any way I would actually be able to establish as fact what I assumed to be true from nothing more than my own informal knowledge?

A reference librarian at New York University guided me to a collection of early Irish-printed books in the National Library of Ireland: the Dix Collection. I expected this collection to be a base of evidence – incomplete, to be sure – of the slow spread of printing there. But it was only when I arrived at the National Library that I began to be aware of the full extent of Dix's scholarship and activity. Not only his collection of Irish books, but also his meticulous chronicling of the first examples of printing in Ireland – books, articles and pamphlets, both published and unpublished – bearing such prosaic titles as *"Early printing in the south-east of Ireland, Waterford," "List of books, pamphlets and newspapers printed in Limerick from the earliest period to 1800," "A list of books, pamphlets, etc., printed wholly, or partly in Irish, from the earliest period to 1820,"* and *"History of Early Printing in Ireland"* formed the foundation of the objective data I needed and led me to other sources. It is not an exaggeration to say that I could not have completed this research or written my first book had it not been for the labors, nearly a century earlier, of E.R. McC. Dix. As an American friend said of him,

He was as familiar with the lives and works of the Dublin printers of the eighteenth century as if they were his contemporaries, and I doubt if there has ever been a bookseller, in even the loneliest corner of Ireland, whom he did not know at least by name.[4]

For nearly twenty years now, I've not only borne an

enormous debt of gratitude to Dix and the many nameless amateur scholars with whom he cooperated, corresponded, and conspired, but I've also frequently found myself wondering, "Who was this man Dix and why did he spend the better part of his life doing all this?"

Ernest Reginald McClintock Dix was born in Dublin on April 8, 1857 to Henry Thomas Dix and Emma Patience McClintock. His father was one of a long line of solicitors extending back to the previous century. His grandfather, William Dix, was both a solicitor and a member of the Solicitor's and Attorney's Yeomanry Corps who was called into service to quell Robert Emmett's uprising in Dublin, 1803.[5] His great-grandfather, Ebenezer Dix, who emigrated to Ireland from England in 1779 or 1780, was also a solicitor, but apparently not as successful as his progeny; he died in Edinburgh, and E.R. McC. Dix notes that "There seems no doubt that Mr. Ebenezer Dix had to leave Ireland owing to financial failure."[6] At the age of 22, E.R. McC. Dix was sworn in as a Solicitor of the Supreme Court of Justice, 3 May 1879, a century after Ebenezer Dix first introduced the family line to Ireland. He spent the rest of his professional life writing and probating wills. But he spent the rest of his personal life chronicling, cataloguing, and collecting examples of books, newspapers, pamphlets, and broadsides printed in Ireland between 1550 and 1850.

Dix did not begin his adult life as an expert in bibliography, although there is evidence of early interest. A typescript monograph that he wrote, "HIDDEN LIBRARIES," undated, is certainly an early expression of his interest in books and the literate environment. In it, Dix writes, "It would be interesting to put on record all existing Libraries whether public or hidden. There are, I believe, small libraries attached to St. Patrick's Cathedral and to Christ Church."[7] The "small library" attached to St. Patrick's Cathedral is, of course, Marsh's Library, founded in 1701 by the Rev. Dr. Narcissus Marsh, Archbishop of Dublin (Church of Ireland). Later in his life Dix would become very familiar with this and other libraries, "hidden" or not, in Dublin and across Ireland and Britain.

In 1884 Henry Bradshaw, chief librarian of Cambridge

University (1867-86), lectured in Dublin about the need to catalogue books, newspapers, and pamphlets printed in Ireland from the earliest days. Like Dix an Anglo-Irishman, Bradshaw had taught at St. Columba's College in Dublin, and had himself presented to Cambridge nearly 5,000 early Irish books and pamphlets that he inherited from his father. It is likely that Dix was present for this lecture, as Robert Welch in *The Oxford Companion to Irish Literature* believes that Bradshaw's exhortation led directly to Dix's founding of The Irish Bibliographic Society and his life-long labors in bibliography.[8]

Some of Dix's fascination with literature and its production and distribution may have been rooted in the cultural ambiguity of the Anglo-Irish experience. As a relatively young man, Dix became involved in the "Gaelic Revival" in Ireland. He was a member of the Gaelic League and at some point before 1897 learned to speak the Irish language.[9] This is not surprising because, as John Hutchinson has pointed out, the Gaelic Revival was a largely Protestant, literate, Anglo-Irish phenomenon, rather than a popular, Catholic, Irish-speaking oral cultural movement. The names most closely associated with the revival – Douglas Hyde, Eoin McNeill, William Butler Yeats – were members of the Protestant, Anglo-Irish ascendancy,

> who, as recent 'settlers,' had a weak ethnic identity that formed gradually out of a series of conflicts, between native Catholics on the one hand and metropolitan Britain on the other...this nationalism was elitist, constructed from written records, and had little hold on the popular consciousness.[10]

The first intimations of Dix's deep interest in Irish printing and Irish books comes in 1898. He wrote a query letter to *The Irish Builder*, a periodical to which he had on several occasions contributed descriptions of castles in and around Dublin.[11] In the letter he described his already growing collection of Irish-printed books from the seventeenth century, and asked readers to write directly to him if they had knowledge of – or actually possessed – other books from that period.

He also wrote a brief article for *The New Ireland Review*, a Catholic journal founded by Thomas A. Finlay, S.J., *Early Printing in Dublin. John Francton (sic), an early Dublin printer and his work.*[12] This was an interesting venue for his debut as an Anglo-Irish bibliographer as Finlay's New Ireland Review had something of a reputation for militant Catholic, Gaelic-Irish nationalism. This paradox is, of course, entirely in keeping with the largely Anglo-Irish Protestant characteristics of the Gaelic Revival.

By 1900 Dix's interest not only in Irish culture but in books and libraries was becoming more publicly known. In a hand-written letter to Eoin MacNeill of December 1900, Dix suggests the establishment of a Gaelic League library and pledged £2 immediately and more if a general, yearly subscription could be established, noting that "(t)he amount at first might be very small but small beginnings sh$^{\underline{d}}$ never be despised."[13]

At about the same time, Dix published his first pamphlet, *Catalogue of early Dublin-printed books, belonging to Mr. E.R. McC. Dix, Dublin,* printed by a publisher called "the Irish Figaro."[14] In the preface to that work, he shed light on his motivations. "The personal fancy or vanity that prompts a book-hunter to print privately a list of his special treasures, needs some excuse, perhaps. Let it be found then in the desirability of having some record kept of our local literature, in case the books themselves should be scattered."[15]

In 1902 Dix wrote and published three pamphlets, two published by the Irish Bibliographical Society. In 1903, Dix wrote – but never published – a "List of Shakespeare's Works Printed in Ireland before 1801," [16] but wrote and published the incredibly helpful *Irish bibliography: A list of Irish towns and dates of earliest printing in each.*[17] He followed that up with *Early Printing in a Munster Town: Ennis,* for the Journal of the Cork Historical and Archaeological Society in 1904.[18] In 1905 he co-wrote (with Seamus Ó Casaide) the definitive work on printing in the Irish language, *A list of books, pamphlets, etc., printed wholly, or partly in Irish.*[19] He produced two pamphlets in 1907, *List of books, pamphlets and newspapers printed in Limerick from the earliest period to 1800,* [20] and *The ornaments used by John Franckton,* [21] and in March of 1908 he was elected a member of the Royal Irish Academy and presented his first paper before that body, *A very rare Kilkenny-printed proclamation : and William Smith, its printer,* which was soon afterwards published in its proceedings. [22]

The year 1909 heralds the beginning of an era of extraordinary activity and productivity for Dix, and of a significant relationship with a new Dublin literary and bibliographical journal established by John Smyth Crone, *The Irish Book Lover*. A pamphlet, *A list of Irish towns and the dates of earliest printing in each,* [23] was followed by four articles for this small but soon-to-be profoundly influential journal in 1909, *The Beaufoy Sale,* [24] *Keatinge's History of Ireland,* [25] *Eighteenth-century Newspapers,* [26] and *The Roundwood Press.* [27] It was also in 1909 that he found, while working tirelessly in the Strong Room of the RIA, "the most interesting discovery I ever made in Irish bibliography, the finding of so many sheets of the Book of Common Prayer" – fragments of the first book ever printed in Ireland – "used as packing for the covers of an old book of tooled leather in the Royal Irish Academy." [28]

1910 saw the publication of eight more articles for *The Irish Book Lover* (at this point, I'll spare the audience the burden of listening to all the titles) and two books, including the still definitive reference work of early printing in the English language (written with H.G. Aldis and Robert Bowes, and edited by Ronald B. McKerrow), *A Dictionary of Printers and Booksellers in England, Scotland and Ireland, and of Foreign Printers of English Books 1557-1640.* [29]

At the same time, we can see Dix's growing network of amateur bibliographers supplying him with leads about previously unknown works or existing copies of works that were known only by their mention in early bibliographies, and supplying leads to sources of books for collection. Some of these correspondences are mordantly funny, as is the letter that arrived on Dix's desk following the deaths of two of his colleagues:

> Sorry to hear of the deaths of Moffett & Waldron. I saw
> the latter mentioned in the press...I hope you'll be able
> to secure some of their books.[30]

I could go on literally for hours recounting the
accomplishments of this obscure Irish solicitor; his donation
of books to small, private libraries in Ireland, as well as the
establishment of the Dix Collection in the National Library
of Ireland; his leadership of the Irish Bibliographical Society;
his election to the board of the Library Association of Ireland,
and his promotion of standards for librarianship and library
education; his global renown as a bibliographer (to the extent
that, in the 1930s, the Librarian of Congress would write to
Dix for information on rare and early Irish-printed books);
and his 150 books, articles, and pamphlets – to say nothing of
the scores of unpublished monographs Dix bequeathed to the
National Library of Ireland.

But in the last few moments of this presentation I wanted
to emphasize once again that Dix was merely the least
obscure in an unimaginably wide network of obscure amateur
scholars, and ask you to consider the meaning of the existence
of such a network. In the final analysis, despite Dix's own
explanation of his motives – "having some record kept of our
local literature" – it is difficult for the postmodern mind to
comprehend the number of people involved, without pay, in
the kind of long-term, deep, and comprehensive research that
Dix's life represents. It is difficult for us to understand that
this was not at all an unusual activity for fairly normal citizens
until less than a century ago. It demanded, of course, a certain
level of education – an education deeply embedded in book
culture. And it may have demanded a certain level of income.
But let us not believe that this was some trivial amusement
for wealthy dilettantes; Dix and his cohorts were solidly – but
nothing more than – middle-class citizens. They were amateur
scholars, but their scholarship has survived to inform the
professional scholarship of the present and the future. If, as
Marshall McLuhan suggests, the "man of letters" is a product

of the printing press, we can expect to see him disappear as the once-dominant press recedes in cultural importance.

Some reading this essay who hold the optimistic viewpoint that new technologies simply by their nature are superior to older ones will try to reassure me (or themselves) that our new media environment guarantees amateur scholarship to an even greater extent than that possible in Dix's time. I will neither speak for nor against this proposition. I expect that it will be questioned in the fullness of time. And I suspect that having been questioned such a point of view will be found wanting. I will merely end paraphrasing some thoughts which ended the book I wrote years ago, a book made possible by Ernest Reginald McClintock Dix: The changeover from one medium to another presents both opportunities and challenges. New technologies empower us, to be sure; but never without some cost which we universally fail to anticipate. We must avoid celebrating the advantages too enthusiastically, lest we miss the meaning of the challenges. For once the changeover is complete, the opportunities and challenges fully assimilated, we will certainly be impotent to undo them.

ENDNOTES

1. Marshall McLuhan, *The Gutenberg Galaxy* (Toronto: The University of Toronto Press, 1962), p. 195.

2. La Tourette Stockwell, "E. R. McClintock Dix: An American Appreciation," The Irish Book Lover, Nov., Dec., 1936.

3. Peter K. Fallon, *Printing, Literacy, and Education in Eighteenth Century Ireland: Why the Irish Speak English* (Lewiston, NY: The Edwin Mellen Press, 2005).

4. Stockwell, op. cit.

5. E. R. McC. Dix, "Annals of the Dix Family in Ireland (Part I)" Unpublished typescript, 1909 (unpaginated); National Library of Ireland, MS 10,663, Seamus O Casaide Collection: Documents Relating to the Dix Family in Ireland.

6. Ibid.

7. E. R. McC. Dix, "HIDDEN LIBRARIES" Unpublished

typescript, undated (unpaginated); National Library of Ireland, MS 8,011 (#1), Miscellaneous Papers and Articles of E. R. McC. Dix.

8. Robert Welch, ed., *The Oxford Companion to Irish Literature* (Oxford: Oxford University Press, 1996), p. 62.

9. Letter to Dix from Seamus Ua Glasaín, 6 June 1897. National Library of Ireland, MS 10,684 (#7).

This letter is written entirely in Irish (Gaelic) indicating that Dix had significant knowledge of the language.

10. John Hutchinson, *The Dynamics of Cultural Nationalism: The Gaelic Revival and the Creation of the Irish Nation State* (London: Allen & Unwin, 1987), pp. 46-7.

11. T. Percy C. Kirkpatrick, *Ernest Reginald McClintock Dix (1857-1936): Irish Bibliographer* (Dublin: Printed at the University Press by Ponsonby and Gibbs, 1937), p.5.

12. E. R. McC Dix, "Early Printing in Dublin. John Francton, an early Dublin printer and his work," *New Ireland Review*, March, 1898. Cited in E. R. McC. Dix, *Printing in Dublin Prior to 1601*, second edition (New York: Burt Franklin, 1971), appendix IX, "Chronological List of Contributions to Irish Bibliography by E.R. McC. Dix," p. 34.

13. Letter from Dix to Mac Neill, December 1900. National Library of Ireland, MS 10,880 Eoin MacNeill Collection.

14. Dix, E. R. McC., Catalogue of early Dublin-printed books, belonging to Mr. E.R. McC. Dix, Dublin : "Irish Figaro" Printing and Publishing Co., 1900.

15. Ibid., p. 4.

16. E.R. McC. Dix, List of Shakespeare's Works Printed in Ireland before 1801. National Library of Ireland, MS 8,011 (3) Miscellaneous Papers and Articles of E. R. McC. Dix – unpublished bibliographies in typescript.

17. Dix (1971) op. cit., p.34.

18. E. R. McC. Dix, Early Printing in a Munster Town: Ennis, in *Journal of the Cork Historical and Archaeological Society*, vol. X (1904), Cork: Curry and Co., Ltd.

19. Dix (1971) op. cit., p.34.

20. E.R. McC. Dix, List of books, pamphlets and newspapers printed in Limerick from the earliest period to 1800 (Limerick: Guy and Co. Ltd., 1907).

21. E. R. McC. Dix, The ornaments used by John Franckton, printed at Dublin and London, 1907.

22. E. R. McC. Dix, A very rare Kilkenny-printed proclamation :

and William Smith, its printer, in Dublin: Proceedings of the Royal Irish Academy, v. 27, sect. C, nos. 6, 7, 1908.

23. E.R. McC. Dix, A list of Irish towns and the dates of earliest printing in each, Dublin: Corrigan & Wilson, Printers 1909

24. E. R. McClintock Dix, "The Beaufoy Sale", in The Irish Book Lover, Vol. I, No. 1 (Aug. 1909), 4.

25. E. R. McClintock Dix, "Keatinge's History of Ireland", in The Irish Book Lover, Vol. I, No. 3 (Oct. 1909), 26.

26. E. M. McC. Dix, "Eighteenth-century Newspapers", in The Irish Book Lover, Vol. I, No. 4 (Nov. 1909), 39.

27. E. R. McClintock Dix, "The Roundwood Press", in The Irish Book Lover, Vol. I, No. 5 (Dec. 1909), 61.

28. E. R. McC. Dix, _Printing in Dublin Prior to 1601._

29. H.G. Aldis, Robert Bowes, E.R. McC. Dix, et al. A Dictionary of Printers and Booksellers in England, Scotland and Ireland, and of Foreign Printers of English Books 1557-1640. London: Printed for the Bibliographical Society by Blades, East & Blades, 1910.

30. Letter from J. S. Crone, 17 January, 1924. National Library of Ireland MS 10,687.

What Neil Postman Thinks About the Internet...

(my imaginary conversation)[v]

Some of my Facebook friends have been having a discussion on the "Neil Postman Appreciation Group" based on a question posed by Bob Berkman: What would Neil Postman say about Facebook, and "scholarly" social networking sites like Academia.edu. Well, I started thinking about it and realized he's already answered the question, several times over. In the last ten years or so of his life, Neil spent a lot of time asking the questions he outlined in his book *Building a Bridge to the Eighteenth Century*. So, in judging the value of Facebook – or of digital social networking in general – we might ask "what is the problem for which Facebook is the solution?"

Imagining the discussion that might have followed when I began to argue with Neil in favor of social networking, I heard these voices:

Peter: Facebook keeps me in contact with people I don't see on a daily basis. Isn't that an objective good?

Neil: What, have you forgotten how to write? Peter, I remember you telling me in 1986, two decades before this MyFace

---

ᵛMany of Neil Postman's statements in this essay are actually his, mostly paraphrased. Some I have invented. But even the ones I invented, I feel pretty confident, are Neil's.

thing–

PKF: No, Neil, it's called "Facebook." You're getting it confused with another social networking site, "MySpace."

NP: (~~sigh~~) Whatever, Peter. You told me about how you wrote letters every week to your cousins in Ireland, about how you were a dedicated – and habitual – letter writer. What happened to you?

PKF: Writing all those letters took a lot of time and a lot of energy. With Facebook all I have to do is send someone a private message and they get it instantly.

NP: These digital technologies certainly deliver information much more quickly than older, "embodied" media. There's no question about that. But does it take any less time or energy to sit and think and write a beautifully-crafted letter – or "message" – on Facebook than it did when you were writing and sending letters through the mail?

PKF: Well, actually, I don't really tend to write as much on Facebook as I used to in a letter. It's usually just a couple of lines.

NP: I see. Why is that, Peter?

PKF: Well, for one thing I tend to "bump into" (in a disembodied sort of way) one or another of my cousins rather frequently online, and we exchange pleasantries almost on a daily basis. Not as much time passes between our moments of contact, and I don't feel as though I have to provide a comprehensive chronicle of recent events. Besides, that's what my "wall" is for.

NP: Uh-huh. And do you share everything on this "wall" of yours? Do you share the same sorts of details of your life on your very public profile page that you once did, in letters, with your cousins?

PKF: Ummm...no.

NP: And so would you say that your interactions with your cousins have changed?

PKF: Yeah, I suppose so. They're far more frequent, but not nearly as deep. But isn't that my fault? You're not suggesting that Facebook has done this to me.

NP: No, Peter, but this is also my point: You have done this. But you have done this with Facebook. Facebook giveth, and Facebook taketh away. You have adopted Facebook as a convenience but told yourself that it is (as you consider all new technologies to be) a necessity. This was a choice involving no coercion or compromise of your intelligence or agency. You have accepted, unquestioningly, your culture's assumptions that, in all matters, but especially those of information, more is better than less and faster is better than slower. And you have accepted this knowing full well (as I taught you) that speed, quantity, and convenience are values in their own right and must compete with other values which you might (because you once did) hold in higher esteem. So you did this, Peter, and you continue to do this, beyond all logic. What's wrong with you? And what are you doing wasting time writing on imaginary walls?

PKF: I don't think you understand the enormity of the change our culture is going through at this moment, Neil...

NP: (~~wry grin~~)

PKF:...I mean, this digital thing is not all bad. It gives us "small people" – as BP Chairman Carl-Henric Svanberg calls us – the power to communicate widely with a potentially global audience. In this sense, it is every bit as revolutionary as Gutenberg's printing press. There has been an enormous proliferation of voices in the last ten years resulting in new ideas and new perspectives that otherwise might never have surfaced in a culture of top-down networks and mass communication.

NP: Sure, Peter, I am aware of that. But to what end? A revolution can be directed toward either a noble or vile end, depending on how one judges such things, just as easily. And Gutenberg had no idea what chaos his press was about to unleash on Europe – and especially on the Catholic Church. Had he known that his machine was about to tear European Christendom into factions that would be at war for the next three centuries he might have thought twice about introducing the world to his "mechanical scribe."

So the Internet is a big deal. So what? To what end does it do its work?

PKF: Huh? Isn't the opening up of channels of communication to enfranchise the information-disenfranchised an end in itself?

NP: I'm not so sure. Do you ever read Jacques Ellul?

PKF: (~~petulantly~~) Yes...

NP: And perhaps a bit of Thoreau?

PKF: Yes...

NP: Well, then you ought to know that our whole approach, as a species, to the relationship between means and ends has changed. Our technologies, Thoreau said, are nothing more than im--

PKF:...improved means to an unimproved end, yes...I know...

NP: Ahem...Yes...and Ellul reminds us that the values of a

technological society present us with a certain...imperative... with which we seem only too happy to conform, namely: to do, to act, to respond, to achieve, to produce, without much regard for what it is, exactly, we are doing, acting on, responding to, achieving, or producing. Technology, as I taught you (and you should have learned by now), answers the human question "how." Ethics answers the human question "why" and it is this question that seems more and more to go missing in our culture. Is giving a voice to those who have none a good in and of itself? Perhaps, and perhaps not. Our culture certainly tells us it is. The values of postmodern, highly technologically-developed "democracies" certainly support this point of view. But isn't it at all instructive to ask, in the first place, whether those who heretofore have had no voice have anything, finally, to say?

PKF: *But isn't this how knowledge increases and spreads, Neil? By opening up channels of information to allow more diverse points of view?*

NP: No, Peter, and I must admit I'm surprised at you for such an elementary error in thinking. This is how *information* spreads, Peter, not necessarily knowledge. Knowledge is another story. To paraphrase Henri Poincare, knowledge is made up of facts, as a house is made of bricks. But knowledge is no more merely a pile of facts than a house is merely a pile of bricks. There is an epistemology at work here, Peter, and a curriculum. And there is a method. Critical thought, based on propositional language, is foundational to the construction of bodies of knowledge. The ability to discern – and reject – useless, irrelevant, and trivial information does not necessarily come easily to the human being. It takes years of hard work and practice to develop the literate mind and the rigors of critical thought. And without these all we have are piles of facts – and in the digital world, truly prodigious piles of facts. Nicholas Carr, when it comes right down to it, asked the wrong question, and in doing so created a straw-man argument that proponents of the digital epistemologies have gleefully attacked and destroyed: will

Google make us stupid? No, of course not! But Carr, in asking the wrong question, missed the point: *human beings evolved stupid.* We're stupid to begin with. Literacy and critical, propositional thought is the therapeutic intervention we invented to cure our stupidity. Writing systems, and particularly alphabetic writing systems, are merely technologies; but literacy and critical, propositional thought are a process, an epistemology, a way of knowing and understanding. Digital technologies, to the extent that they provide us with a shortcut to "information" (again, without regard to the quality of the information) that bypasses these thought processes, don't make us stupid, but counteract the therapies that we ourselves invented to ameliorate our stupidity. Epistemology, curriculum, and method cannot be separated without consequence.

So what digital technologies have done, perhaps, in empowering the information-disenfranchised (as you call them) is not to have spread knowledge, but to have spread stupidity.

PKF: But many of my friends and colleagues insist that these digital technologies support propositional thought, that people are reading more as a result of the internet, and kindle, and iPads, and all the other various venues and applications. Can you deny that?

NP: I can neither confirm nor deny that, and I'll confess to you that I hope – and pray – that it is true. But I'll also confess to you that I have my doubts and remain skeptical about such suggestions based on my observations of human behavior, especially where technology is involved. It was one of Marshall McLuhan's last public acts to identify a set of "laws of media." One of these so-called "laws" was his observation that every medium taken to its furthest extent flips to its opposite. Of course, McLuhan didn't mean this. A tool is a tool, a piece of metal and plastic with some wires. It is we who revert to an earlier form, *we* who flip into our opposites. Despite the deep faith of your friends and colleagues in electricity's ability to preserve literacy, the written word, which is the source of all the intellect we have, when pushed to the speed of light, when used to churn out new, sensational, untested pieces of incoherent, decontextualized information for sale in a marketplace, becomes a medium for the expression of all our stupidities.

PKF: Why do you say that, Neil? Isn't that a bit harsh?

NP: Peter, are you aware of what the two most widely used applications of the internet are?

PKF: Ummm...yes, as a matter of fact.

NP: Well? What are you waiting for?

PKF: E-mail and pornography.

NP: Yes. Virtually 100% of internet users have one or more active e-mail accounts. Nearly 70% of internet users download and view pornography. Now, don't think I'm a prude, Peter (many people believe I am, you know, and worse – a reactionary!). I'm not condemning people for engaging in an expressive form that is as old as the species. It just serves as an illustration of my point. Given a medium (one that is, in a sense, the accretion of all previous media) that allows for engagement with both propositionally-structured information and presentationally-structured information, people will choose titillation, excitement, and amusement every time. Reading is difficult work and unnatural; sensory experience is not. I'm reminded of Christine Nystrom's article – you remember Christine, don't you?

PKF: Of course I do. She was my dissertation chair.

NP: (~~annoyed~~) Oh, yes. That's right, she was. Well, anyhow, I'm reminded of something she once wrote called "literacy as deviance." Her point was that human beings invented writing and eventually printing only because we were, at those points, insufficiently technologically advanced to invent television. All of human technological development, she suggested, is aimed at constructing tools that more and more accurately mimic human sensory experience. Hence, our infatuation with "virtual reality" (as though actual reality were not real enough), and her observation that alphabetic writing was merely a detour on this path. At any rate, whether you call it an iPad, or an e-book, or a schmindle, what you're really talking about is a computer hooked to the internet. Come to think of it, what kind of environment are we living in when you can make phone calls on a book? But I digress. As long as we're talking about computers with multiple applications, only one of those being to access text, we're very likely, I believe, to find that people will use them to look at pictures or movies, or listen to music just as frequently as – if not more than – to read text. There are, of course, the other issues of what we're reading (to go back to our earlier discussion of information) and how we're reading (if you wanted to discuss Sven Birkerts's ideas of the profoundly interior experience of "deep reading"), but I think you get my point. I am skeptical about the ability of digital technologies to support the epistemology, curriculum, and method of print culture. Extremely skeptical.

PKF: Listen, Neil, my friend Robert Berkman wanted me to ask you a question...

NP: How long have you known Bob Berkman?

PKF: Well, we've actually never met, but ---

NP: So why do you call him your friend? Look at how new technologies do violence to our language!

PKF: Well, he's a Facebook friend...I know it's not the same thing, Neil, but, look, he's a nice guy, he's smart and asks good questions, suggests good answers -- and his profile picture always has a smile!

NP: Just get on with it, Peter. I don't have all day. I'm playing Bridge later with McLuhan, Innis, and Ong...they're all *terrible* at basketball...

PKF: Well, Bob thought you might be more amenable to giving your approval to sites like Academia.edu...
NP: Academia what? What's that? That's a new one to me...

PKF: It's a website for scholars. You have your own page – a profile page that links to personal information, research interests and activities, etc. Other scholars can "follow" your work, and you can upload your research and get comments from other scholars.

NP: (~~shaking his head~~) That sounds like an *awful* idea. Why in the world would you want to do that?

PKF: Well, again Neil, it's this idea of opening up channels of communication, getting reactions from diverse perspectives, generating synergy...

NP: Synergy, schminergy, Peter. You're talking gobbledy-gook here. You sound like some marketing hack tossing about trite advertising slogans. I warned you about "word magic" after you handed in your first research paper at NYU, remember? Don't puff up your thoughts with fancy-sounding words to make them appear, to those who don't know any better, more important than they really are. Peter, let me ask you a question.

PKF: (~~red-faced~~) By all means.

NP: You've written a book now, correct?

PKF: Ummm...actually, Neil, my second book just came out. It's called "The Meta --

NP: Yes, yes, whatever. My point is, did you write this book by yourself, or did you organize a committee to write it for you?

PKF: I wrote it myself, Neil, but there were a lot of things I was writing about that were, quite honestly, beyond the boundaries of my expertise and personal and academic experiences. I found it both useful and necessary to have the manuscript read, at various stages, by philosophers and theologians to make sure I was moving in the right direction.

NP: And did you find these philosophers and theologians on Academia.edu?

PKF: No.

NP: No? Why not?

PKF: Well, I don't know most people on that website --

NP: You don't know Bob Berkman but you call him your friend...

PKF: But that's Facebook, and that's different. What we're talking about now is--

NP: -- MyFace with another name.

PKF: (~~not daring to correct him again~~)

NP: You didn't put your work up on Academia.edu for comments, and you wouldn't have accepted comments or criticisms that were offered on Academia.edu because you don't know who is leaving them. Oh, you may see their names there, you may even be able to check their "credentials" – certainly, we can trust all the information the Internet provides, right? – but that doesn't mean you "know" them. Instead, you found your readers where?

PKF: Oh, these were people I knew personally and respected. These were people who others know and respect too.

NP: Another question, Peter, beyond the specific issue of specialized response. You didn't write chapters of this book and post them to get others' responses?

PKF: No.

NP: If you had, would you have modified or changed your manuscript in any way?

PKF: No.

NP: Why not?

PKF: Oh, simple: this was my book based on my ideas. I've had this experience before in conversations about this book, and about the perspective from which I wrote it. People can't touch my data, but they hate my conclusions. We get into arguments about "the meaning of it all," and, at the end of the day, people are just resistant to points of view that stray too far from their comfort zones. I thought about posting excerpts on Academia.edu, and in fact did post excerpts on Goodreads.com – which is more interested in literary merit than scholarship – but decided to avoid Academia.edu. I thought there'd be too much pressure to conform to more mainstream points of view.

NP: You can tell Bob Berkman that I agree. My books, for better or worse, have all been mine. Tell him he can keep his AcademiaBook, or MyFace, or whatever new thing pops up. Pen, paper, and trusted colleagues with whom to talk are all I've ever needed. If you're smart you'll allow the bare necessities to sustain you too. Now go, Peter, and sin no more…

(Anyway, that's how I imagine the conversation going...)

We're All Trayvon Martin

The Trayvon Martin case has touched a very raw nerve in American culture. After years of being hidden away in the closet of the American mind, the spectre of racism once again haunts us. Ever since the 1960s – the "Freedom Riders," the civil rights movement, the march on Washington and Dr. King's stirring speech at the Lincoln Memorial, the march from Selma to Montgomery, the passage of the Civil Rights Act and Voting Rights Act – Americans have been convinced that racism is a thing of the past in the United States of America. Since the election of Barack Obama as President of the United States, many Americans have indulged in bouts of smug self-congratulation or reassured themselves that – no matter what is in their heart – they can no longer be accused of racism.

It's not that easy. That's far too easy.

There's no question that the attitudes of average Americans changed during this time. Where white Americans once either ignored the group of people we once called "negroes" or thought about them as somehow less than human, the civil rights movement of the 1950s and 1960s was very likely helped by the emergence of television. Images of men, women, and children in peaceful protest being beaten with truncheons, attacked with dogs, and swept off their feet and blasted with fire hoses, brought home to America the injustices of inequality. The powerful, emotional images entering our homes night after night sparked our sympathy for Americans of African descent and changed our minds about accepting the status quo of Jim Crow segregation.

Of course, all of this changed in the 1980s and 1990s, with Ronald Reagan's deregulation of the television industry, the rise of the FOX News Channel, the 1987 abolition of *the Fairness Doctrine*, and the growing power of talk radio. Reagan's Federal Communication Commissioner Chairman Mark Fowler redefined the principle of public service for broadcasters with a free-market context. The FCC, he said, "should rely on the broadcasters' ability to determine the wants of their audience through the normal mechanisms of the marketplace. The public's interest, then, defines the public interest."[1] No longer would one group's – any group's – quest for equality *necessarily* be a news story; no longer would inequality, injustice, disenfranchisement, prejudice, disparities in employment, education, or wealth *necessarily* be a news story. On the contrary, this type of "bad news" would be relegated to "the back of the bus" in terms of coverage while mass media delivered more salable, more attractive, more palatable distractions to their mass audiences.

The rise and growth of cable television meanwhile – and FOX in particular – appealed to niche interest groups and "narrowcasting" information became more prominent. FOX itself has become a staple in the homes of conservative Americans; indeed, four out of five self-described "staunch conservatives" watch FOX at least occasionally, and more than half watch it regularly.[2] FOX's success stems from the fact that their viewership receives information that validates their worldview, information – ideas and opinions – that was not necessarily available within a mainstream, broadcasting context.

In the late 1980s, following the FCC's (under Mark Fowler) abolition of *the Fairness Doctrine*, AM radio, displaced in its older role of music delivery by FM and high definition digital audio formats, became a haven for conservative "talk" shows, carrying a mix of news, opinion, and phone-in discussions. Right-wing "personalities" such as Rush Limbaugh, "Dr." Laura Schlesinger, Laura Ingraham, Glenn Beck, Bill O'Reilly and others helped to create a milieu in which an extreme right-wing world view was not only acceptable, but affirmed and reinforced on a daily basis.

Now, I'm pretty certain that anyone reading this essay who happens to be white will vehemently – angrily! – disagree with me, but we're fooling ourselves. Ask a white American, liberal or conservative, what he or she thinks of racism, and they will tell you just how awful and inhuman it is. Ask a white American if he is racist and he will be shocked – shocked! – at the suggestion. "I am not a racist," he will tell you. "I have black friends." But, I repeat, we are fooling ourselves. No one wants to think of himself as racist any more than he would think of himself as stupid or ignorant or hateful. But stupidity, ignorance, and hatred are in no short supply in the United States in the second decade of this new millennium. But certainly, they are somebody else's problem; you must be talking about them. It's not me.

Racism did not disappear from our nation in the 1960s. It merely went into temporary hiding. Racism, now officially banished from public policy and cultural norms of acceptable behavior, disappeared from our words and actions. It lives on, however, alive and well in our hearts. Certain words have disappeared (we all know the words I'm referring to). Certain behaviors have disappeared. We now consider the words vile and disgusting and the behaviors boorish and uncivilized. And even "conservative" talk show hosts can lose their jobs when they cross a line that is socially unacceptable. Ask "Dr." Laura.

But have we changed? Have our hearts changed?

A lot of the problem stems from our understanding of the words "racism" and "hatred." It's very easy to have a friend, black or white. Friends are people we like. We like them because we believe they're good, and we believe they're good because we've bothered to get to know them, to know their hearts. I have black friends and white friends and Asian friends and Latino friends. I have Christian, Jewish, and Muslim friends. My students are black, white, Latino, Asian, Christian, Jewish, Muslim, and atheist. I can honestly say I love my friends. And I can honestly say that I love the vast majority of my students (if I have a problem with a student, it would be more connected with their seriousness and work ethic than their ethnicity). They are, like me, American. Does that mean I am not a racist? Again, it's all a bit more complicated than that. Nothing is that easy.

Rather than preaching and laying blame elsewhere, let's start with me. If I am walking down a Chicago street late at night and a young black man wearing a "hoodie" is walking toward me, am I uncomfortable? Why? I neither know the young man nor anything about him. I have no reason to believe that he has any intention, good or ill, other than to walk down the same street I am walking. What could possibly be the reason for this discomfort?

Human beings tend to fear two things: 1] that which they don't understand, and 2] that which they *think* they understand, if they understand it incorrectly. And here's where racism comes in. Very few (if any) Americans will admit this, but we all have preconceived notions of others based on social categories. We react to people that we don't yet know *not* as individuals, but as members of one of these categories. And we make decisions about what category people belong to based on their appearance. This is the essence of stereotyping. We all do this. All of us. There was a brief period in American history, from the civil rights movement through the 1970s, when there appeared to be a chance to attenuate the spread of stereotypes; but new information outlets narrowcasting niche viewpoints has made prejudice socially acceptable again.

I have written in the past[3] about both white racism and black racism (what some white people refer to as "reverse racism"). And I said I understood black racism far more than I understand white racism. I said that white racism is based on deeply-seated feelings of privilege and cultural superiority, and "reverse racism" (black racism) is based mostly on resentment of white privilege and on fear – fear of someday being a victim of white racism. Like Trayvon Martin.

And here's where hatred comes in. In order to hate, it is not necessary to actually take a gun and shoot someone. It is not necessary to beat someone with a club until unconscious, chain him to a pickup truck, and drag him around town until his lifeless body literally falls into pieces. In order to hate, it is not necessary to make someone sit in the back of a bus, give him a separate bathroom, or make him step off the sidewalk as you walk by. In order to hate someone, it is not necessary to call him a vile and disgusting name.

All that is really necessary to hate someone is not to give a shit about what happens to him. And when we don't give a shit about what happens to a whole group of Americans because of the color of their skin, *that is racism*.

So I feel it necessary to point out the following inconvenient truths:

- On average, African-Americans have a lower life expectancy than white Americans, with higher infant mortality, greater risk of coronary artery disease, diabetes, stroke and HIV/AIDS.[4]
- African-American unemployment is on average twice the white unemployment rate, at all times, not just during the current economic crisis.[5]
- At some point in their lives, 42% of African-Americans will experience poverty as opposed to 10% of whites.[6]
- One third of black children live in poverty today compared with 15% of white children.[7]
- Black Americans experience homelessness at a rate seven times that of white Americans.[8]
- 70% of white high school students go on to college as opposed to 55% of black students.[9]
- A black man is three times more likely than a white man to be stopped and searched by police (racial profiling), and once stopped is four times more likely to encounter physical force by police.[10]
- A black man is nearly 12 times more likely than a white man to be sent to prison on drug charges, even though the greatest number of drug users is white.[11]
- Young black students are three times more likely to be arrested than white students.[12]
- If and when arrested and convicted, black prisoners spend about 10% more time in prison than white prisoners.[13]
- A white man who kills a black man is far less likely to face the death penalty than a black man who kills a

white man.[14]

- Someone of any race who kills a white man is four times more likely to face the death penalty than someone who kills a black man.[15]

And most of America doesn't give a shit. Not about any of this. On the contrary – if we're going to be honest with ourselves – we rather expect that this is pretty much "just the way things are." We like to tell ourselves that in America "anyone can make it if they try," that all you have to do is "pull yourself up by your bootstraps" and "work hard to get ahead." In other words, if you are one of the 45 million Americans living in poverty, you're just not trying hard enough. And if the majority of that 45 million is black – well, the numbers speak for themselves, don't they? As Herman Cain said, "If you're poor and unemployed in America, *blame yourself!*"

White Americans will never admit it, but deep in their hearts they still believe that black people are inferior. And any attempt to point out the disparities and injustices in our social and economic structures, any attempt to suggest that there are structural inequalities built into the system that we have *never* addressed, any attempt to argue that racism survives in America – these are all met with the charge of *"race baiting!"*

None of this is ever going to change until each of us changes. The change has to come *from* us, and the object of that change *is* us. We have to change our hearts. And we have to change our minds. We have to stop thinking in terms of stereotypes and deal with people as people. We have to stop thinking in terms of narrow self-interest and begin to reclaim the idea of *the common good*.

A week before he died, The Reverend Dr. Martin Luther King Jr. preached at the National Cathedral in Washington DC. He called his sermon "Remaining Awake Through a Great Revolution." In it he said the following:

We must all learn to live together as brothers or we will all perish together as fools. We are tied together in the single garment of destiny, caught in an inescapable network of mutuality. And whatever affects one directly affects all indirectly. For some strange reason I can never be what I ought to be until you are what you ought to be. And you can never be what you ought to be until I am what I ought to be. This is the way God's universe is made; this is the way it is structured.

John Donne caught it years ago and placed it in graphic terms: "No man is an island entire of itself. Every man is a piece of the continent, a part of the main." And he goes on toward the end to say, "Any man's death diminishes me because I am involved in mankind; therefore never send to know for whom the bell tolls; it tolls for thee." We must see this, believe this, and live by it if we are to remain awake through a great revolution.[16]

Trayvon Martin's tragic death is bigger, I think, than a debate over a really bad self-defense law ("stand your ground"). It is bigger than our own narrow political agendas. It is bigger than our bruised egos when someone accuses us of racism. It is bigger than the terrible, incompetent justice system in a small Florida town. It is about something bigger than all of these, I believe; Trayvon Martin's killing touches on something universal. His death ought to make us look at ourselves and be honest: we need to realize that no one in America is safe until everyone is safe, that no one in America is a success until everyone is a success, that there is no more central a self-interest than the interests of all.

George Zimmerman didn't hate Travon Martin. He didn't even know him. He hated some *image* that Travon looked like in Zimmerman's ignorant, image-addled brain. He didn't kill an innocent kid; he killed a stereotype. And that stereotyped thinking has to stop. The responsibility is white America's. When white people *finally* see people who don't look like them as equal, when they stop looking at the Trayvon Martins of the world as "thugs" and "gangstas" and treat each individual human being as a person (as, by the way, Christ taught us to do), then people of color, immigrants, Muslims, and other groups suffering discrimination will be able to see white people as people too, and not as dangers to their safety. Gandhi once said, "I like your Christ. I don't like your Christians." Well, I love America. But there are too many hateful Americans. The way I see it, we're all either Trayvon Martin or we're George Zimmerman. The choice is ours. There's no in-between.

ENDNOTES

1. Brainard, Lori *Television: The Limits of Deregulation* (Boulder, CO: Lynne Rienner, 2004), p. 61.

2. Pew Research Center for the People & the Press *Beyond Red vs. Blue: POLITICAL TYPOLOGY* (Washington, DC: Pew Researech Center for the People and the Press, 2011), p. 42. Accessed May 23, 2012 from http://www.people-press.org/2011/05/04/section-3-demographics-and-news-sources/

3. On my personal Blog, *IN THE DARK*, on March 24, 2012. http://rujournalism.blogspot.com/2012/03/were-all-trayvon-martin.html

4. Smedley, Brian, Michael Jeffries, Larry Adelman and Jean Cheng, *Race, Racial Inequality and Health Inequities: Separating Myth from Fact* (National Association of County and City Health Organizations and California Newsreel, 2009). Accessed May 22, 2012 from http://www.unnaturalcauses.org/assets/uploads/file/Race_Racial_Inequality_Health.pdf

5. Algernon Austin, *Unequal unemployment—Racial disparities in unemployment vary widely by state* in Economic Policy Institute. Accessed May 22, 2012 from http://www.epi.org/publication/ib257/.

6. National Poverty Center, *The Colors of Poverty: Why Racial & Ethnic Disparities Persist* (Ann Arbor, MI: National Poverty Center, Gerald R. Ford School of Public Policy, 2009), p. 1.

7. Ibid.

8. U.S. Department of Housing and Urban Development, *The 2010 Annual Homeless Assessment Report to Congress,* U.S. Census Bureau, 2010 American Community Survey; Institute for

Children, Poverty, and Homelessness, *Inter-generational Disparities Experienced by Homeless Black Families* (New York: The Institute for Children, Poverty, and Homelessness, 2012), p. 1.

9. Restituto, Nicolas Miller and Gerald Miller, *Education and Racial Inequality* (Kansas City, Mo.: Rockhurst University, 2005), p. 5. Downloaded (.pdf file) May 24, 2012 from http://cte.rockhurst. edu/s/945/images/editor_documents/content/PROJECT%20 INEQUALITY%20STUDENT%20PAPERS(Listed%20 Alphabetically%20by%20P/rest.pdf

10. American Civil Liberties Union, *Department of Justice Statistics Show Clear Pattern of Racial Profiling* in aclu.org. Accessed May 23, 2012 from http://www.aclu.org/racial-justice/department-justice-statistics-show-clear-pattern-racial-profiling

11. Do Something.org *11 Facts About Racial Discrimination* in Dosomething.org. Accessed May 25, 2012 from http://www. dosomething.org/tipsandtools/11-facts-about-racial-discrimination-0

12. St. George, Donna *Federal data show racial gaps in school arrests* in The Washinton Post: National. Accessed May 25, 2012 from http://www.washingtonpost.com/national/federal-data-show-racial-gaps-in-school-arrests/2012/03/01/gIQApbjvtR_story.html

13. Quigley, Bill *Fourteen Examples of Racism in Criminal Justice System* In The Huffington post: Politics. Accessed May 25, 2012 from http://www.huffingtonpost.com/bill-quigley/fourteen-examples-of-raci_b_658947.html

14. Death Penalty Focus, Racial Disparities. Accessed May 25, 2012 from http://www.deathpenalty.org/article.php?id=54

15. Ibid.

16. King, Martin Luther, Jr. *A Testament of Hope: The Essential Writings and Speeches of Martin Luther King, Jr.* (New York: Harper Collins, 1986), pp. 269-270.

Peter K. Fallon is Associate Professor of Media Studies at Roosevelt University. A veteran of more than two decades in television, Fallon left NBC News in 1999 to teach at Molloy College in New York in their Department of Communication Arts. His 2005 book *Printing, Literacy, and Education in Eighteenth Century Ireland: Why the Irish Speak English* is the winner of the Marshall McLuhan Award for Outstanding Book in 2007, and his second book, *The Metaphysics of Media: Toward an End to Postmodern Cynicism and the Construction of a Virtuous Reality*, won the Lewis Mumford Award for Outstanding Scholarship in Technology for 2010. Fallon recently completed a two-year term as editor of *EME: Explorations in Media Ecology*, the international scholarly journal of the Media Ecology Association.

Made in the USA
Middletown, DE
05 January 2021